ISBN 978-1-61808-170-4

Printed in the United States of America

White Feather Press

Reaffirming Faith in God, Family, and Country!

Contents

The

Bastard

Curse

Illegitimate Faith:

A Perspective of the Downfall

of America and the Church

Pastor Wayne North

Acknowledgements and Thanks

I would like to thank God for His love and commitment to me through the redemptive work at Calvary. I am humbled by his empowering mercy and grace to be able to do all things through Christ, and the continuing transformational work of the Holy Ghost. I would like to thank my wife and family for their input, prayers and support, as well as my spiritual family at FREEDOM Community Church. All have recognized my calling and gifts that extend outside the local church and have encouraged me to follow God's anointing in my life. I also want to say a special thanks to Pastor Dale Smalley and his wife Lin for their example of a couple totally sold out to Jesus Christ and His will.

Introduction

The series "Why Not?!" was given to my wife through the inspiration of the Holy Spirit, and is dedicated to a vision that focuses on "Why Not?!" So many people are blindsided by the consequences of their choices. "Why Not?!" places our hope and success firmly upon our faith in Jesus Christ. The series, "Why Not?!," is a prescription and an antidote for a world saturated with sin, and its consequences and the hopelessness it leaves in its path. "Why Not?!" concentrates on the kingdom of God and His cure for those spiritually helpless, homeless and hurting. My hope is that this first of the series, and those following, will provide thought-provoking, commons-sense analysis discussion and interventions. Furthermore, it is my goal to outline the strategies for spiritual maturity and eternal success founded upon the powerful Gospel of Jesus Christ.

We see dozens of churches close their doors each day. We must ask ourselves "WHY?" We see tens of thousands of people walk through the doors of Mega churches only to remain the same as they were before they came to Christ. We also must also ask ourselves "WHY?" As we are evangelizing only less than four percent of the U.S. population we must ask ourselves

"WHY?" As we see a culture that has a one percent Biblical Worldview we know the church is dying. In fact, many churches are DEAD spiritually even though they have thousands of members. They just have great programs. In the western church, we do not rely upon God, especially the Holy Spirit, for sustenance and viability. Our society, including our churches, have become self-centered and entertainment driven. We have killed transformations in favor of information. We have settled for numbers rather than truths. We have focused on the needs of man and his favor rather than pleasing God and seeking His favor. We cannot earn His love or salvation. But scripture states that He desires obedience. We can earn His favor and blessings. God's eyes search across the earth for righteous hearts and lives. So many people are asking "WHY?." Believers continue playing "weekly" church either in the small or Mega-churches, believing God did away with His precepts and Laws and believe God is okay with sinful lifestyles. Many can't believe how fast sin and perversity are consuming our society, observing the prevalence of darkness overtaking the earth and how days are getting worse.

I have decided, rather than focusing only on the WHYs, we should be walking out our faith by exclaiming "WHY NOT?!" Scripture says these things must happen. We continue to run the race and "let not our hearts be troubled." If we believe Christ is who He said He is and the Holy Spirit will do what He says He will do, we will press on and be empowered to do even greater things through Christ. Not because of us but because of the One who lives inside us. The same Spirit who raised Christ from the dead, and empowered Jesus to do the will of the Father, has empowered us to follow in His footsteps and the disciples, and their disciples, and ... So WHY NOT?!

WHY NOT ... LIVE A HOLY LIFE?

WHY NOT ... BELIEVE IN MIRACLES?

WHY NOT ... PREPARE PEOPLE FOR THE NEXT STEP?

WHY NOT ... BE A COUNTER CULTURE?

WHY NOT ... BE REAL AND RELEVANT?

WHY NOT ... PRESENT THE ONLY TRUTH?

WHY NOT ... RAISE THE GREATEST GODLY GENERATION EVER?

WHY NOT ... BE BOLD?

WHY NOT?! ... WHY NOT?! ... WHY NOT?!

Dedication

I dedicate this and all my success to God, and those He has placed in my life that challenge, encourage and refine me to be able to do far more than I could ever dream or imagine through Christ's power and kingdom principles.

Deuteronomy 23:2 A bastard shall not enter into the congregation of Jehovah. Even to his tenth generation he shall not enter into the congregation of Jehovah.

Zechariah 9:6 And a bastard shall dwell in Ashdod, and I will cut off the pride of the Philistines.

Dedication

I dedicate this and all my success to God, and those He has placed in my life that challenge, encourage and refine me to be able to do far more than I could ever dream or imagine through Christ's power and kingdom principles.

Deuteronomy 23:2 A bastard shall
not enter into the congregation of
Jehovah. Even to his tenth generation he shall not enter into the congregation of Jehovah.

Zechariah 9:6 And a bastard
shall dwell in Ashdod, and I
will cut off the pride of the
Philistines.

Chapter 1

The Bastard Curse

THE BIBLICAL DEFINITION OF BAStard from Strong's Greek and Hebrew Dictionaries:

H4464 ממזר mamzêr mam-zare'
From an unused root mian. to *alienate*; a *mongrel*, that is, born of a Jewish father and a heathen mother

G3541 νόθος nothos *noth'-os*
Of uncertain affinity; a *spurious* or *illegitimate* son

A synopsis of Merriam-Webster's Dictionary's definition of Bastard:

an illegitimate child; something that is spurious, irregular, inferior, or of questionable origin; lacking genuineness or authority; whoreson

We live in a culture of illegitimate relationships and people, but God has placed a heavy emphasis upon covenant relationships. His promises endure forever. He made many different covenants with man. Even all of creation is within covenants. A bastard child is one conceived or born outside the covenant of marriage. Many of our relationships are outside the covenant of God. We think it doesn't matter who our friends are, or what we do or ... in fact, it does. A covenant has very stringent requirements. A bastard child has many issues most of which come from not having a Godly covenant of protection from conception on. We live in a culture where couples live together before getting married (fornication.) Most of these relationships fall apart. Human relationships should be the opposite of test driving a car. We are formulated to have deep relationships with one another. Curses travel from one generation to the next. The above scripture states out to the tenth generation. WOW! Does this alarm you? Maybe you don't believe we have spiritual issues to deal with. Yet, we, as the Body of Christ, are as illegitimate in our walk as anyone else.

As we continue to buy into the "free" sex promotions societal consequences continue to worsen. Sexual sins are the most devastating sins carrying the heaviest consequences. I believe this is why the depression, suicide and mental health issues are sky rocketing. We are giving away the purity that God reserved for us. It is NOT ours to give away outside the bonds of marriage. Parents who encourage their adolescent children to get a boyfriend or girlfriend for "recreational dating;" thank you for destroying the next generation. Thank you for destroying your child. Not only your child but other children as well, and even the next generation and beyond. "Free" sex is not free! It costs us everything! Decades ago there were only four types of STDs. According to the Medical Institute for Sexual Health, we now have at least 27 types of "STIs", many of which are incurable and symptomless. No cost, right? And that does not include the suicides because of the consequences of harlotry in our society. A common term that may be offensive is slut. We have many male sluts and female sluts walking around. Purity and character are left behind as we see a culture of innocence being lost.

As with physical and relational illegitimacy, spiritual illegitimacy also runs rampant in our churches and society. We do not have a clear view of the gospel of Jesus Christ. We see it through selfish, "Greekish" eyes of intellectualism and enlightenment. We slam preachers who add to the word of God foretelling of their future BBQ in the Lake of Fire. Yet, most people remove scripture from the Bible with no problem. Proclamations that He doesn't work that way anymore, or God has changed somehow, or that was for the first century church, cloud the working of the Holy Spirit.

> Mark 3:29 But he who blasphemes against the Holy Spirit never shall have forgiveness, but is liable to eternal condemnation.

We produce illegitimate spirituality by not developing personal relationships within our church families, both small and large. We do not covenant together. We do not cover each other. In fact, we really don't know that person near us in the pew or chair. We have lost the definition of community even within our faith communities. Try maintaining, let alone building, a family by meeting one day a week. Maybe at the most two days a week for a few hours. It can't be done! People have lost the Biblical Worldview.

Questions to ponder:

1. Define what a bastard child is?

2. Why do you think they will never find a place to rest or belong?

3. What does the Holy Spirit do?

4. Why do you think blasphemy of the Holy Spirit is so severe?

Chapter 2

The Natural Realm

We TRULY LIVE IN A FALLEN world. Adam and Eve had the cloak of authority placed upon them by God Himself; they were commanded to subdue the earth and be fruitful and multiply. The only limitation was that they could not eat from the Tree of the Knowledge of Good and Evil. This tree was reserved for God. He was to retain this knowledge. As a good parent, He knew how to protect His children. It didn't take long before the "jealous one" attempted and succeeded in tempting them both to take the forbidden fruit. Adam, who was given the restriction allowed Eve to take the first bite. Then he joined her. Maybe he wanted to see if she would die first. The rest goes down in history.

All because of this one treasonal act, all of creation fell. There were consequences of man's actions that started the decay and destruction of creation. Why do I call this a treasonal act? Well, God's government is based upon a kingdom foundation. The King declares it. The people obey it ... OR ELSE! In this case, all of creation will pay for man's disobedience. But, we would have done the same. I am sure of it.

I believe man was created to live forever when God made him in his own image. He breathed His life into man. In fact, He breathed His Spirit into man. After the fall, man lost "life." The life in the garden. The life in his marriage. The life in his work. The life of his career. The life of his relationship with the King of kings, and Lord of lords. Adam and Eve realized they were naked and were ashamed. I am sure they hid because they felt disobedient and that God would reject them. Things would not be the same as they knew it. Shame, guilt and condemnation would saturate their minds in this new, fallen world.

Little did they know, that thousands of years later, the consequences would be continuing to expand and explode in the creation around us. Adam and Eve were more interested in the stuff than a relationship with the "stuff" creator. Maybe you could say that because fruit has high sugar content, they were looking for more of a "sugar daddy" than a daddy. Our world today is no different.

that intertwine with the roots of other vegetation and trees. The soil of faith will have the right nutrients that will grow us. We must root our faith into soil of Jesus Christ. Then, we will grow. Moreover, we will flourish and reproduce this DNA in others. After all, the purpose of maturity is to reproduce.

As I farm, I must test the soil, pick the right seed, add the right nutrients, till the soil, kill the weeds and root them out. These are some of steps needed for a crop to be produced. The last step is to harvest the crop when it is ripe and mature. Many things are out of my natural control throughout the growing season. This is where I apply my faith. I pray to loose the rain, and to bind up the storms. My spiritual preparation of my crops is just as important as the physical preparation. I have literally watched storms split and reform on the other side of the field. What a faith builder!

We were destined by God to be planted and flourish. I never plant my crops on the farm to lose money. Our worldly desire is to prosper. Yet, we get hammered by the spiritual community for a desire to flourish. God's definition for my flourishing is sovereign. It could mean financially, emotionally, spiritually, in favor, in miracles or in any combination of these, or all of these. All I know is that something will happen. I anticipate God's favor upon my life for being planted and seeking righteousness.

I am writing this book not to the world, but to the professing Christians around the world. Even more precisely, I am writing to the western culture, and then, the church in the United States. My heart ripples throughout the ends of the earth for the lost not to perish, but to come to salvation through our Lord and Savior Jesus Christ. Yet, these ripples must first start where I have been plopped. We must prosper where God has planted us.

Psalms 92:12 The righteous shall flourish like the palm tree; he shall grow like a cedar in Lebanon.

Psalms 92:13 Those that are planted in the house of Jehovah shall flourish in the courts of our God.

I grew up farming with my family and continue farming to this day. We've lost a lot of translation built within nature and the universe around as we've become less rural and agricultural. Built within the seed is the DNA that it will need to grow into whatever the seed has been called to be. The acorn has all the DNA it needs to grow to be that mighty oak tree, able to withstand the droughts and storms in life. It needs to be planted to get the nutrients to accomplish this growth. If we are truly planted, we become the righteous. Therefore, we should become the strong cedars of Lebanon. We will develop strong root systems

What Adam and Eve lost in the garden, Jesus restored spiritually through His death, burial and resurrection. He defeated the kingdom of darkness.

> 1 John 3:8 He who practices sin is of the Devil, for the Devil sins from the beginning. For this purpose, the Son of God was revealed, that He might undo the works of the devil.

Jesus wasn't only a servant when He came the first time. He put the "smack-down" on the works on the devil. A common chemical used in farming today is glyphosates (for example, Roundup ®). Glyphosates kill the plant including the roots. Roots tend to re-grow the plant if they are not killed. Glyphosates take care of that problem. Jesus wants to kill our sin down to the roots. The roots are the cause and sustainer of the "weed" (sin) in our life. Thus, just pulling the leaves and stem that is above ground will not kill the weed.

Our spiritual life works the same way. Most of the world, including the church, treats only the symptoms. In future chapters, we will be looking at divorce, anger, homosexuality and suicide. Many of these are like having cancer and treating only the pain. We need to get to the roots of the problem. The church has lost its relevancy in the world. Our role is to be ambassadors for Christ. We are His ordained and anointed sons and daughters who continue the example He set while He was on earth. Jesus taught His disciples, His ways, and commanded them to pass these on to the next generation.

> John 14:12 Truly, truly, I say to you, He who believes on Me, the works that I do he shall do also, and greater *works* than these he shall do, because I go to My Father.

I believe the church has lost its first love. The church has lost its focus, purpose and passion. It has become a nice religion that boxes God up, and it allows for man to be in control. When we whole-heartedly seek after Jesus, we will see miracles, deliverance, Fruit of the Spirit, Gifts of the Spirit and Salvations. We belong to a kingdom ruled by the King. Yet, we fail because we operate in a democratic mindset. He rules and reigns over us as His church. Church is so much more than preaching, teaching and music. Church is a natural presence of a supernatural congregation. We are to be the church. People are the church. It is about God, then people. Jesus' whole ministry was to bring the kingdom of God to the hearts of men.

> Matthew 9:35 And Jesus went about all the cities and villages, teaching in their synagogues, and preaching the gospel of the kingdom, and healing every sickness and every disease among the people.

Luke 9:2 And He sent them to proclaim the kingdom of God and to heal the sick.

Luke 10:9 And heal the sick that are in it, and say to them, The kingdom of God has come near you!

Luke 17:21 Nor shall they say, Lo here! or, behold, there! For behold, the kingdom of God is in your midst.

Luke 11:20 But if I cast out demons with the finger of God, no doubt the kingdom of God has come on you.

Because the church lost its first love, we've lost the kingdom power of Jesus Christ: the power that transforms lives; the power that sets the captives free; the power that heals the sick and delivers the oppressed from demonic torment. Man has replaced God's power with entertaining services and religious traditions. People who are afraid of God "ruining" their self-built kingdoms, misuse their positions with control, fear and intimidation. This makes as much sense as me cutting off my cornstalks and some of the ears of corn to make sure I can handle the harvest. Rather than adapting to the harvest, we manipulate the harvest (if any) to our capability. Our capabilities stink! In fact, many of the people controlling others have very dry walks. Have they led someone to the Lord recently? Are their prayers being answered? Do they see miracles happening? Have they assisted in the deliverance of someone from demonic activity? Have they healed the sick? I know it is the power of God that does these things! BUT, he chooses His vessels, US, to accomplish this in His name. Moreover, these people who are diseased with anger, malice, control, hatred, depression, and pride lack the foundational Fruit of the Spirit founded upon Christ and the Spiritual Gifts that follow. What a shame!

It is time for the generations to rise up. It is time for the army of Christ to rise up to meet the challenge of this decaying world. The Truth hasn't changed. The need for the Truth hasn't lessened. We must worship Him in Spirit and in Truth. His Spirit empowers us to be His supernatural hands and feet. Out of our lips come blessings or cursings. Let us bless and love the people who are drowning in the spiritual garbage and consequences of this world.

We live in a world where illegitimate relationships, families and communities are being reproduced all around us. The term "bastard" encompasses the need for real and relational activities to be fostered all around us. Even our churches for the last fifty years have been suffering from the cancer of illegitimate reproduction within our society. The church has been a sub-culture of the world, rather than a counter-culture of truth and hope. The church lags behind by about twenty years.

Whatever is popular in the society will become popular in the church. We have let the culture determine truth. While sometimes we reach out and speak the language of the culture to get the Truth across, many times we change the Truth to meet the culture.

Questions to ponder:

1. What tree have you been picking the fruit from lately?

2. Has God ever removed the blinders off your eyes so you could see your nakedness of sin?

3. What are the signs and symptoms of the church losing its first love?

4. What lies have been reproducing in our church culture that now have become truths because they have been told enough?

Chapter 3

The Results Don't Lie

WELCOME TO THE UNITED STATES of Socialistic America. Some of you may disagree, or even get offended by that statement. Yet, as a science and math educated man, I tend to apply the scientific method when it comes to problem solving. The last step in the scientific method is the conclusion. After collecting data from the experiment, a person quantifies the results and attempts to explain the relationships. I see the world and society continue to spiral downward. Failure of the family, society and government become more evident. Socialism replaces God as the answer and the "giver" of rights. The government becomes God and demands cohesion to its values and political correctness. It "enlightens" its substituents to its progressive ideas, and the archaic principles that are founded upon people with a narrow, closed-minded thinking. We must look at the history of the world and the failure of these man-centered institutions.

The Bible says that there is nothing new under the sun. So, it is easy to see that the effects of sin upon the world demand God's attention. Sin demanded a response from God in the garden, before the flood, and upon Sodom and Gomorrah. The list even points to you. Your sin has demanded a response. Even before your birth, God already responded to your sin. He sent His Son, not only as a response, but as a cure for sin. At some point, God will respond to those who did not respond to His cure (confused yet?) In His righteousness, He cannot let sin into His kingdom. Since His kingdom is in the heart of man now, His plan is for us to live a holy life NOW! Not by our might, nor our power, but by His Spirit. Jesus anoints us with His authority to be His ambassadors. The Holy Spirit empowers within us the authority of Jesus Christ. Yet, sin demands a response. Moreover, sin brings a curse here on earth. I believe the devil knows scripture better than we do. He might understand his rights to torment us (because of sin) better than we know our rights. Through the inheritance from Jesus Christ, He strengthens us and has made us victorious over the power of the enemy. The enemy works through the works of deception, fear and ignorance.

Proverbs 26:2 As the bird by wan-
dering, as the swallow by flying, so
the curse without cause shall not
come.

In scripture, we are encouraged to choose life,
which to me means we could choose the opposite:
death. Sin opens the door of torment, curse and other
negative consequences. I believe everything good
comes from heaven, and everything bad comes from
the fallen world and the realm of darkness.

Is it a wonder why, when the courts removed the
openness of one to pray and read the word of God in
school, the schools themselves started to disintegrate?
Just like creation started a slow decay because of sin,
the school started to reap what it was sowing. At the
university level, there has been an outcry by the pro-
fessors about the level of cheating and plagiarism.
Don't they realize that what they have been teaching
for a generation is now the "truth" of the next generation. The educational system has pushed for relative
truth. They teach that no one's truth is better or worse
than another's. They strived for rebellion and rejection
of parental values and especially Christian values. The
generations listened very well. Their truth allows them
to do whatever it takes to succeed. University staff
should be proud of their response, but they didn't expect the culture to apply what they taught back upon
them.

Likewise, we see a government that seems to believe they own the children. Both in the educational and medical systems we see a degradation of what used to be a fundamental right for parents to raise their children. This is revealed in cases presented in "overruledmovie.com." Government institutions are deeming what is right and wrong for our children. This is similar to what the Nazi party did in the 1930s. The plan was to separate the children from the parents. Camps were created to teach and nationalize the children's views and attitudes. Occasionally the children would head home to visit. The problem was that the children who were indoctrinated with the hogwash of lies soon turned in their parents to the government as anti-Germany "terrorists. " Anyone against the current vision is a terrorist and enemy of the state. Sounds familiar doesn't it!

It appears as if the right for parents to educate their children has turned into the right for the state to indoctrinate their children. Home schooling and private schools are the enemy to the social agenda of the anti-American movement. Better yet, the movement is toward a one world government against the freedoms of the people, and especially against Christianity. A Biblical Worldview is dangerous and threatening to the slavery mentality of the liberal agenda. Yes, I used the word slavery. A person must see the connection between a socialistic agenda and post modernism culture. Many believe religion has killed more people than anything else. But, truth be told, atheism and secular humanism are about as inhumane and destructive as one can get. The nineteenth and twentieth centuries were littered with leaders destroying the hopes and dreams of individuals through the lies perpetrated within socialism and communism.

Jesus came to set the captives free. Whom the Truth sets free is free indeed. Jesus is about freedom. Not the freedom to do anything you want, but the freedom to choose truth, and certainly not the freedom to be free of the consequences of making bad choices. He empowers us to be overcomers and conquerors. Christianity is not about the do's and don'ts. It is about relationship … relationship with a God that has sought us out. He came to us first. Other religions either have us trying to be god or trying to find god somewhere. What a joke!

Our culture has begun to embrace the idea that being rich, poor or in-between is bad. Our culture has been playing "class" warfare for decades now, or much longer. Their view is that if they can make us enemies of each other, they can step in as the heroes of the day, and make us all equal. But isn't that what the Declaration of Independence states: "We are all equal?" No, it says we are all created equal and have rights given to us by our Creator. Yet, because of our choices we are not all equal. Abortion points that out. Liberals for the freedom of choice, which murders the freedom of the unborn, have no problem removing the rights of groups they feel are less important or valuable.

We live in a culture of sin and death. They go hand in hand because sin leads to death. Even the Ten Commandments tell us of the consequences of sin.

> Exodus 20:5 You shall not bow yourself down to them, nor serve them. For I Jehovah, your God am a jealous God, visiting the iniquity of the fathers upon the sons to the third and fourth generation of those that hate me,

> Exodus 20:6 and showing mercy to thousands of those that love Me and keep My commandments.

We live in a culture where the sins (iniquities) of the fathers are passed to the children. Alcoholism, abuse, disease, anger, poverty, divorce and sexual deviance are all areas where we see it become generational. In fact, we see each generation fall deeper into the darkness of depravity. I have seen verbal abuse in one generation turn into physical abuse in the next, which turns into self-abuse in the next and leads to suicidal tendencies including homosexuality in the next. Sin has consequences. Perversity has consequences.

Yet, we also see blessings passed on to the next generation, out even to the thousandth. We must see that God's laws of goodness always triumph over evil.

Light always overpowers the dark. The key is rooted in love and obedience. We cannot love God without obeying Him.

I grew up observing the Sabbath. I have encountered many Christians that have wanted to accuse me of being a legalist. Yet, most of them tell their counterparts that they must go to church too. Legalism isn't rooted in Saturday or Sunday; it is rooted in the heart. Many say following His heart (commandments) is legalism. I disagree! Legalism occurs anytime we "have to" rather than I want to. Any principle God ordained and commanded must be important, or we are calling Him legalistic too. Many act as if the Father went through anger management classes before He sent Jesus to earth. Jesus is love, but not the Father? God has not changed! He is very clear about His heart. We are to love what He loves, and hate what He hates. Obedience is not legalism. Legalism is in the heart.

The Pharisees were not confronted by Jesus for being obedient to God's word, but for their disobedience. They were accused of telling everyone else what to do but it was far from their heart. They were doing their own thing and not God's. They were tyrants of the day. They were sons of the devil.

> 1 John 3:4 Everyone who practices sin also practices lawlessness, for sin is lawlessness.
>
> 2 Thessalonians 2:8 And then the lawless one will be revealed, whom the Lord shall consume with the breath of His mouth and shall destroy with the brightness of His coming,

We live in a culture that embraces God's love but not His righteousness. God is! He has not nor ever will change. Many churches and people say they are "New Testament" churches and people. What happened to the "Whole or Complete Testament" church? We must resist any temptation for a culture to mutate the Truth. Cancer is a mutation of healthy cells. Truth sets the captives free ... free from the consequences of sin and lies ... free to live out the calling and rights endowed by our Creator. True freedom doesn't occur when we can do whatever we want. Freedom occurs when we minimize the effects of the consequences of sinful choices. Only God empowers us to live a life free from these consequences. Embrace God's ways, and resist the ways of the world. The results don't lie!

Questions to ponder:

1. Do you see a correlation between Nazi Germany or even the Roman empire, and the USA?

2. Are we all equal?

3. Lawlessness and legalism are equally bad. Which one do you deal with the most?

4. Obedience and Freedom are equally good. How do you seek these elements out in your life?

5. Who is the lawless one?

Chapter 4

Physical and Spiritual

Cultures of Divorce

WE LIVE UNDER A COVENANTING God. Creation was part of a covenant. The flood was too. Marriage is the best example of a covenant that is sealed in blood. His promises are sealed in blood, the blood of Jesus Christ. As believers, we are called to be in the covenant. I also believe that in churches we are to be in covenant to one another. A covenant is promise and contract of what we will invest, sealed by the Holy Spirit with the blood of Jesus.

But, look at the culture of divorce we live in today. When divorce became 'no fault' back a few decades ago, the divorce rate skyrocketed. Some statistics show the divorce rate around 50 percent for first marriages, 65 percent for second marriages, 80 percent for third marriages and around 97 percent for fourth marriages. Wow! For decades now we've had a culture of covenant breakers. In fact, divorce within the professed Christian community could be higher than the secular stats. I have heard that the African-American community has 80 percent of its homes fatherless. Other ethnic groups are catching up too. No wonder our culture is inundated with gangs and pseudo-family cultic activities. We have young men growing up without the needed guidance of a father, causing these young men to gravitate to the ditches of violence (to prove their man-hood) or homosexuality (in an attempt to deny their man-hood.) Furthermore, these men not only make up the vast-majority of our prison systems (80 percent), but I feel are much more likely to abuse youth and children causing these youngsters to struggle with their identity. In the very least, these immature "men" will reproduce physically, emotionally and spiritually other immature "men."

We have created a culture of children and adults that have no real identity or foundational family relationships. We live in a culture where our children are pushed away and devalued. Right from birth, babies are described as masses of tissues similar to tumors or warts. Our culture has warped our minds by the dating cancer. Our children are taught that they must date and be sexually active to get whatever they can from the other person. Selfishness abounds! We all are taught that the other person should make us happy or we should move on. What a lie from the pit of hell! Once a couple has pre-marital sex, on average, that relationship will last about three more weeks. Men have been taught to conquer. Once they conquer, they move on to a new challenge. As a teacher in the public schools, many times I watched as the boys picked off the innocents of many young ladies. At that point the girl many times falls into the cycle of one relationship after another, always trying to regain her identity and self-esteem, only to delve deeper into heartache and despair. Having a discerning spirit, I break when I look into the empty eyes of the young women (and even men) lost in loneliness and rejection. And as they have children, this lifestyle and "cancer of the soul" is mentored to them.

We have the same issues inside the church. We live in a relationship-free culture. Everyone seems to live in superficial relationships. Self-protection is evident and fostered. Many walls of protection are fortifying the hurt and deep brokenness of their hearts. The average size of the church in America is still under 100, probably under 50. Yet, more and more mega-churches are rising-up out of the quagmire of sin and offense in our culture. Not only has the vast-majority of churches left their first love, Jesus, they have traded His truth for a politically-correct, powerless gospel of demons. Scripture is very clear about not even associating with such teachers. We are commanded to flee from even the appearance of evil, so we are to leave such churches. But, this is not why most leave.

Most leave churches because of boredom, offense, and lack of commitment. All these invalid reasons show the condition of the heart and its immature nature. For these reasons churches no longer teach the meat of the word, or even the whole scripture in order to retain their immature visitors. The main purpose for many churches has been changed from making mature disciples into making simple converts. In fact, in our culture, it has almost become impossible to disciple because of the curse of not belonging (the bastard curse.) In fact, we see churches that are led by spiritually superficial pastors, worship teams and teachers. In my area, I know of churches that tolerate spiritual leaders who get drunk on a regular basis as well as using illegal forms of drugs on a regular basis too. No longer do we have to study to show ourselves approved. All we need to do is to have a gift and say we are a Christian. Again, the problem is this: those leaders will reproduce people just like themselves. When a new person walks through the door of the church we must test the fruit of their lives. Their fruit will "minister" more than their gifts.

As a teacher, I have noticed that generally when tragedy happens in a child's life like divorce, the child stops or drastically slows their maturing process. This can be true physically, emotionally and spiritually. In the healing ministry, we many times have to take the person back to the age and time of the incident and attack the root of the problem there. I have seen 70-year-old men hanging on to words their fathers spoke over them that caused hurt and destruction. In our culture, the children are forced to make more mature decisions with less spiritual and emotional substance. Decades ago the average age of maturity for young men was 18-21 years of age. Today it has been estimated that it is 27 years of age and climbing. More and more 20- and 30-year-olds are lacking initiative to balance faith, family and career. In fact, I feel most can't do one of these ... period!

The culture of divorce has been subsidized by the "nanny state," where "children" can stay on their parent's insurance until they're almost 30 years old, and where people can get on disability because they can't get along with others. Where there are no expectations, people will no longer strive for integrity and excellence. Remember the Jewish culture where the boys were expected to become men in their teens? Now teens are expected to play all the time. I like to have fun as much as anyone else, but when I became a man I had to put away childish things.

In fact, technology has added to the issues. Because of the divorce culture, people communicate at a lower grade of communication. No longer do we communicate, we just talk at other people. Most forms of communication are "billboard" in nature. Most technology-driven communication lacks body and facial expression and language. People from divorced families struggle more with relational issues. So, they become obsessed with hobbies, sports and video games. Symptoms of ADD and ADHD, along with obsessive-compulsive behaviors become more evident within our culture. People who lack control try to obtain it by going overboard. I think most people would agree their lives are out of control or too busy. While we need to stop and smell the roses and to be thankful in all things, I see most people overemphasizing the "me" time. Again, we don't need more recreation in our society, we need more re-creation. God needs to transform us daily. We must submit to His ways and plans.

The more we 'rec-reate' (verses 're-create',) the more empty we feel. It becomes like a drug. I personally struggled with my hobbies of hunting and fishing. If I couldn't do these every day, I felt empty. They consumed me and my time. Something that God created to allow me to enjoy life, became a black hole that stole my life. In fact, most of the things I enjoy can consume people. A dear friend and brother in Christ who has decades of coaching, and with great success, told me that very seldom does sports or any other activity teach you character. Generally, these opportunities allow you to show your character. Your character will be revealed in hardship and struggles. Great coaches never develop players, they develop people. The huge movement in our society is towards competition. Parents, because they can't parent or are weak in it, hand their children off to others to let them raise their children. A culture of divorce precedes a culture of hopelessness and despair. Loneliness and self-gratification abound. Remember, Hitler almost took over the world by destroying the family and the church. He took the children away from the family and church and indoctrinated them in schools and national camps.

I thank God for a loving family, a praying church and a loving wife. Otherwise, I would have been one of those statistics. But, it still pains me to watch this generation be consumed by the things of this world. As the Body of Christ, we are to be in the world, but not formed by (of) it. I recall the parable of the ten virgins: five were wise and five were unwise. All of them were virgins. To me this meant they abstained from the evil of this world. They did not yoke themselves to the evil. In other words, sex makes a soul tie. I believe God was very intentional in the verbiage of "virgin." The virgins abstained from connecting with evil, and all ten were waiting for their groom to come along. There was anticipation by all of them. After all, the purpose of remaining a virgin is wrapped up in the anticipation of the one you are waiting for to come and the two becoming one. It also appears that all ten had some form of light, but only half of them prepared for a delay. We live in a culture of the unwise virgins. In fact, most "Christians" aren't even virgins when it comes to the things of this world. The new and improved Christians "feel" we aren't restricted any longer by rules and regulations of the mean God of the Old Testament. After the Father had a Son, it changed Him. Or maybe He got with the times and realized He was being a little old-fashioned. Or maybe He got some anger management classes and learned how to deal with His control issues. Or maybe He could blame it on not having a father Himself. Yes, I am being sarcastic! From the beginning of time, and probably before, He has always had the same plan. He wants to redeem His creation back to Himself. He wants relationship with His children. He wants family. He doesn't need us … He wants us. WOW! Get that through your head. All that He does is out of a love for us. All the commandments and judgments exist to create a loving relationship between Him and His children.

The virgins all thought they were going to get married. Yet, they failed to walk in the preparation of perseverance. I feel the oil here represents the anointing and sealing of the Holy Spirit. Sin isn't just doing the wrong thing; it also isn't doing the right thing. We are told that those who endure to the end shall be saved. We can see the correlation between us and Israel. They too thought they had the title of the chosen people, the bride. Yet, in their disobedience they must also come through faith in Jesus Christ and His atonement for their sins. In fact, God divorced them, only to "remarry" them again. We must abstain from evil and also do good. Out of our salvation we work. We work out our salvation with fear and trembling. Work it from the inside out to the outside. Many Christians are like the five unwise virgins. They feel they have abstained from evil. They know Jesus is coming. Yet, have they been empowered by the Holy Spirit to do good? Have they been preparing themselves for the Groom? It appears that just believing in Jesus and His return will be enough. After all, demons believe in Jesus. But, they tremble in His presence and at the mention of His name. We don't! Are they wiser than us?

Most Christians don't want to be virgins when it comes to the things of the world. We have the rebellious spirit inside us that drives us to try it, or we must learn for ourselves, or everyone else is doing it. In a culture of divorce, these thoughts and attitudes are the norm. Most values used to be taught at home. But since there is no home, or family, or Godly parenting, the children have become orphaned to the world, government and society. All these institutions fail to teach values, and cannot give meaning and purpose to each individual. In fact, these three culprits perpetuate despair and meaningless value through their only "gospel:" the "gospel" of evolution. What an irony? Evolution teaches that there is no design or purpose. Everything is a random mutation that ends in death and more chaos. Evolution ultimately arrives at hopelessness and despair for all who are brainwashed by its religion, but the "gospel" of Jesus' good news arrives at hope and joy.

Questions to ponder:

1. What devastations has divorce caused in you or your family's lives?

2. Much of the technology we have today creates a division within one's self, let alone within the parts of the family. What effects have you seen because of technology?

3. Most of our choices push us and our families into fantasy realms and artificial roles in life. What can we do to stop our houses and families from being divided?

4. Which type of virgin are you in the parable? Both were looking for the Bridegroom, but only one got to meet Him.

Chapter 5

Church Life,

or is it Death

AS WE SEE A CULTURE ADHERING to the lies of a movement to discredit scripture and the eternal truth of Jesus Christ, we contemplate it "cancer" within the church. We have spoken briefly at times of what is happening in the church. We are approaching the perilous times spoken of in scripture. Much of the world has seen it much more than we have here in the USA. Men have become lovers of themselves. We see mankind calling good evil, and evil good. We see a culture of immaturity growing within the church. We see the family breakdown destroying the purpose of a spiritual family within the local church. We see people church-hopping looking for the next fix or running from the pain of offense. We see a church culture of going to church rather than being the church of Christ.

Some claim these things are typical in church life, but would we be more correct in saying the death of the church. Maybe it's God's plan to kill the church, to raise it from the dead. Maybe only then will a remnant come forth that is relentless and fervent for His Kingdom. Persecution brings about revival ... so does suffering and financial struggles. For revival to break out maybe we should be praying for persecution, suffering and struggles. We have the option to be revived in the good times but we are much too busy having a good time to worship the good God.

Worship has become about music rather than lifestyle. Therefore, we argue about worship style and forget about lifestyle. What we do 24 hours a day, seven days a week is much more important to God than the pseudo-worship used to entertain man for one to two hours on Saturday or Sunday. Would we not rather entertain God than man? Would you rather please God or man? We cannot serve both God and man. We cannot serve two masters. Through our submission to God we serve man, but we will never serve God by submitting to man. One brings life, the other death. Who do you serve and please? Because who you serve and please is who you worship!

I challenge my church all the time to pull out your checkbooks or your calendars, and we will see what god you serve. People say, as I once did, that they can't afford to tithe. God says you can't afford not to tithe. They also say they have no time to go to church. God says choose this day whom you will serve. But, most people will still not grow by only going to church. The purpose of going to church is to gather the saints. The church service is the locker room chalk talk for the big game. Practice time can be both individual and corporate as we study, pray and worship. But we all come together to work together on the "field" or "court" of life. The real game is out on the streets and alleys in the world. Our mission field is our family, jobs, friends and even enemies. So why are we failing?

See, when we look at the body of Christ we see a body that is divided. AND not so much from each other as much as we are divided from the Head. We can have no life apart from the Head: Jesus Christ. Many in the church want a relationship with the written word, when it is the Living Word that we need to have "connection" with. Just like in battle, when you cut off the head, the leaders, you place the rest in chaos. Where does vision come from? The head, specifically the eyes.

> Proverbs 29:18 Where there is no
> prophetic vision the people cast off
> restraint, but blessed is he who
> keeps the law.

The head gives us vision. The head gives us revelation. In fact, we are to put on Christ and the mind of Christ.

> Ephesians 4:22 to put off your old
> self, which belongs to   your former
> manner of life and is corrupt through
> deceitful desires, and to be renewed
> in the spirit of your minds, and to put
> on the new self, created after the
> likeness of God in true righteousness
> and holiness.

We remove ourselves from the old self by dying to it daily and letting Christ raise us out of the grave of our self. We must walk in the newness of life. Most people who come to Christ in our culture make a little "guest" room in their soul for Him to live in. He doesn't want a room, He wants the whole "house" of YOU! As we are transformed by His glory.

> 2 Corinthians 3:18 And we all, with
> unveiled face, beholding the glory of
> the Lord, are being transformed into
> the same image from one degree of
> glory to another. For this comes from
> the Lord who is the Spirit.

It is my personal opinion, with respect to scripture, that we are either owned by God, or owned by the devil. Put another way, we are either possessed by God

or the devil. No way around it, one of them owns our soul. We are changed by the Spirit who lives within us. Every day by His power and glory, we should become more like Christ through the process of sanctification. God brought you out of "Egypt." Now He needs to remove the "Egypt" within you. It's much easier for us to change the outside. He wants to change the inside which will then change the outside. The outside will seldom cause an internal change. So what is the key?

The key is the molder and shaper of who we are. Either we are conformed to this world because it has molded and shaped us, or we have been transformed by the King of the Universe. Transformation is like the caterpillar morphing into the butterfly, except we are to have a different DNA. The caterpillar has the same DNA as the butterfly. Butterflies lay fertilized eggs that produce more caterpillars. Physical laws show that two deer will only produce another deer, not an eagle. Spiritual laws follow a similar pattern. We can produce only what we are. So many times in counseling, I hear the words like, "I use to struggle with "X" addiction before I had kids and knew Jesus, so why do my children struggle with it now?" See, the devil knows his rights. Externally we may have changed the "X" problem, but have we really defeated it at the cross through Jesus Christ? Have we truly submitted it unto the glory and under the blood of Jesus Christ? It is the power of the Holy Spirit that changes the DNA of our family line. It is my opinion, based upon many years of working in counseling, healing and deliverance ministries that people don't really deal with their sin issues.

I liken this to buying a house and having the renters refuse to leave. I must exercise the authority of the law to remove them. The same is true in the spiritual realm. I see in scripture that through the blood and name of Jesus Christ I have been empowered as an ambassador of His kingdom to speak His authority. Ambassadors speak upon the behalf of the one who sent them as if the king/president himself were there saying the words. What an awesome and humbling responsibility. Many transfer the "title" of their "house" over to Jesus Christ, but don't ask the previous "owner" to leave. Therefore, the children walk in the same sinful footsteps, if not worse, as the parents. If we haven't been transformed into a new spiritual DNA of Jesus Christ, our old sinful DNA will still reproduce new sinful DNA. I love science because all of creation points to the nature of God. Even in its fallen form, nature points to a creator. Scripture is clear about the analogy between conforming versus transforming.

> Romans 12:2 Do not be conformed to this world, but be transformed by the renewal of your mind, that by testing you may discern what is the will of God, what is good and acceptable and perfect.

The separation between the Head of the church,

Christ, and the body of the church, us, is clearly illuminated by the above scripture. There is an epidemic of confusion in our culture today even within the church. People are all over the board when it comes to who they should marry, as well as if and why they should go to college. The church is just as chaotic. Most people take their life and ask for God to fit around us. God wants us to take our life and mold it around His sons life. We need to reunify the body back to the head. We must be transformed by the renewing of the mind. And then through the tests we will discern the will of God. His will IS good, acceptable and perfect!

The problem is that to behold His glory means to walk in His presence. We must walk in His footsteps. We can't be transformed by the world's ways or activities. It is only by the power of the Holy Spirit that we can transform into His likeness. We must choose transformation or conformation. After all, His way are not our ways, nor His thoughts our thoughts. BUT, we can attain His ways and thoughts by the process of transformation. The question will change from "what can I do and still be saved?" to "what does He want me to do to become more like Him?" See, we got it wrong. Holiness comes from the inside and it must translate to the outside.

It's interesting that the outside of our body is basically made up of dead cells that help protect us. See, we must die to protect ourselves. Once we die, life will grow out of it. Death to our will, protects His will for our life. The other interesting fact is that within every cell of our body is a nucleus, the cells brain, made up of the same DNA that the Head has. So, the Head of the (church) body directs the body. Not just the organs, or the tissues, but the cells (individuals.) The body is made up of many parts each with purpose and a destiny. AND when one part of the body hurts, it affects the whole body. If one part of the body is infected, the infection can become systemic and kill the body. This is why God warns us:

> Proverbs 6:16-23 There are six things that the LORD hates, seven that are an abomination to him: haughty eyes, a lying tongue, and hands that shed innocent blood, a heart that devises wicked plans, feet that make haste to run to evil, a false witness who breathes out lies, and one who sows discord among brothers. My son, keep your father's commandment, and forsake not your mother's teaching. Bind them on your heart always; tie them around your neck. When you walk, they will lead you; when you lie down, they will watch over you; and when you awake, they will talk with you. For the commandment is a lamp and the teaching a light, and the reproofs of discipline are the way of life,

God hates these things because they become systemic and hurt, even destroy, His children and His reputation. God will not be mocked! We will reap what we sow. If we sow discord within the body, we will reap strife (discord.) Then they will be divided and will become more bitter. We are commanded to let grace abound. Love covers a multitude of sin. Yet, we are unwilling to forgive those who offend and hurt us. That sin then falls upon us. We are also commanded to forgive because He forgave us.

The body does not think for itself. Even in our reflexes, a signal is sent to the central nervous system (likened to the Holy Spirit) and a pre-programmed response is given. The nature of God ruling in our hearts causes us to pull away from even the appearance of sin. (We are to flee.) The sin nature causes us to draw nearer to sin and the things of this world. What is running your spiritual central nervous system? It will cause either life or death. The same thing happens at the bigger level within our churches (likened to the tissues in the body.) Are the members in the local body encouraging and carrying one another's burdens? Are the spiritual gifts at work to bless one another? Is forgiveness running rampant, or is offense and unforgiveness consuming us? The list runs on and on. Does your life bring life to others, or does the darkness of your heart bring darkness to others?

The DNA of Life will reproduce life in others. The

DNA of sinful death breeds death to those around us also. What DNA are you reproducing?

Questions to ponder:

1. Is your life like the rich young ruler or one like Paul's or Peter's? (Matthew 19:16-30; Mark 10:17-31; Luke 18:18-30)

2. Prophetic vision and keeping the law seem to go hand in hand in Proverbs 29:18. Explain how this can be.

3. It appears we are commanded to be transformed.

    What does this mean?

4. Someday, you will be required to have a blood test before you enter heaven. Will you be carrying the blood of Christ in and upon your life, or will you try to enter upon your own blood's merits of sin and failure? Let Jesus transform you by His blood in your life!

Chapter 6

Church Symptoms vs

World Symptoms

WHENEVER A SCIENTIFIC STUDY is done, there is usually a control group and a test group. The test group will get the so-called drug and the control group would get the placebo drug (no drug.) In the results a conclusion would be reached on if the drug indicates that it improved the disease. Applying this to the church vs the world, we the church has the cure for any and all sin (disease). The world is the control. They continue in their sinful ways. The problem is that we now can't tell the difference between the results between the church and the world. In fact, at best because there has been that division between the head, Jesus, and the body, us, the church resists any change but usually within a few years accepts the cultural shift. We have seen this with slavery, alcohol, divorce, fornication, homosexuality, lying, ...

Scripture states "to come out of her (the world)". He was the salt of the world. We have been called to be the salt of the world. We have been called to be "cure" for the world. Not us, but the One who lives inside us. If the capsule represents people, the stuff in the capsule represents the things that fill us. Some are filled with nothing. They feel empty. They offer nothing to the world around them. In fact, because they know they are empty, they build up the walls of their capsules. Their walls become hardened. If they did not, the cares of the world would cause them to implode. The pressure of the outside world would be greater than the pressure pushing outward. Empty capsules are weak, and pointless. If you have ever had an empty capsule because the ingredients weren't put in, or came out, they are easy to recognize. That was not what they were created for, so they are discarded, thrown aside. People empty on the inside are many times discarded by society because people are valued only by what they can offer. These people are so empty they do themselves and others no good.

Others are like capsules that have been filled with the things of this world. They represent the placebo drug. Within the capsule there is a "sugar." Things that taste good are easily burned up. They don't offer any hope, treatment and definitely no cure. People taking placebos think they are getting the possible cure. They have the positive thinking the world says they need to have to cure themselves. Yet, like in the treatment of cancer, sugars are what the cancer feeds on. Therefore, even the placebo worsens the condition. What people think tastes good, will ultimately hurt them, even kill them. The lie I hear a lot is, "the goal in life is to be happy." Hogwash!!! This explains why marriages fall apart. The spouse doesn't make them happy anymore. So, it's time for a new one. What a burden to place on someone! We cannot make someone happy. We can only help draw the best out of someone. Happiness is more of an attitude than a feeling. Feelings come and go. True happiness comes out through rejoicing. We are commanded to rejoice in all things. We are commanded to give thanks in all things. Rejoicing lays the ground work for happiness to grow. The feeling of happiness will come and go like the seasons. Joy can remain. Yet, most people will never experience real joy because they are filled up with the world's placebo for true joy. The world says sex, drugs, money, power, and hard work will make you happy. It will be like a temporary high, short lived and harder to achieve the next time. And the high after that, ...

People want a fix, more than a fixing. Hundreds of time I have watched people choose temporary solutions for lifelong issues and eternal sinful actions. Jesus Christ has wanted nothing more than to transform our lives into His glory. He has never been into being a genie in a bottle. Christians want that genie more than God. Again, most anyone who declares such things as "you don't have to go to church to be a Christian" have turned God into a genie. They want the power to manipulate Him. When they need something, they will modify their lives marginally in order to manipulate God into doing their will. Yet, Jesus even said that, " not my will, by Thy Will (the Fathers) be done on earth as it is in heaven. We are more concerned about our will than His.

The true disciples of God have Jesus in their heart. Their capsules are filled with the Holy Spirit. The Holy Spirit represents the One Jesus sent upon His behalf to save the world. He is the only hope for the "cancer" of sin in our lives. So, what does He bring? He brings holiness and obedience through love. He empowers us to say no to sin and yes to holiness. People not filled with the Holy Spirit live the same way they always have, even if they admit to having asked Jesus into their hearts. He just doesn't want an invitation, He wants the title to your heart ... the abstract. The ownership and control is to be handed over. We should start acting more like Him, even in our non-perfect bodies. Without holiness, no one will see God. Some say it's His holiness. Yes, but we must put it on and walk into it. As He loves His followers, we will too. True believers love hanging out with other believers.

People who are true believers will long to minister *with* and *to* other believers. The placebo Christians are already filled with other stuff. They have the same 24 hours a day as everyone else. We all choose how to spend it. Most of our time determined not by commitments, but choices. Just like most of what we have is the wants in life, so is how we choose to spend our time. We are called to empty ourselves as an offering. Marginal Christians, at best, make excuses of why they don't get plugged in. It goes back to the Bastard Curse. Their life is grounded and rooted in rejection, offense, condemnation and hopelessness. They are the first to complain that Christians are judgmental. Yet, it is their judgment that hurls the first stone. I said it before, it takes a judgment to decide if you feel your being judged. So, let us get over it.

People receiving the real cure will begin to change and get better. Their disease will be destroyed. Those taking the placebo, or wrong drug, will stay the same or gradually get worse until death. Where am I? Where are you? It may be time to get the real deal. Jesus said that He is the Way, the Truth and the Life. No other way to God or to heaven. Even though our politicians and social deviants want to determine what is acceptable and okay, they can never vote someone into heaven or into salvation. God has determined that it takes repentance to accept the totality of Jesus' sacrifice and empowerment leading to life. When people truly come to Christ the empty capsule is filled. The placebo drug is emptied out and the cure is poured into them. Then, and only then can the Cure (Jesus) defeat the sin in your life. Quit looking for a fix, and find the Fixer! Each of us are led astray by our own selfish desires and sinful tastes. Die to ourselves, pick up our crosses and follow Him. Jesus came to give life and life more abundant.

How many of us are living the abundant life? The church has become a New Testament church without the Old Testament God. That is why we moved from pharisaical religion to lawlessness. Again, I will emphasize that the Old Testament was and is just as important. All of it is God's plan and attributes of His character. We live in a lawless society and church, because most believe the God of the Old Testament changed. What was reserved for a few in the Old Testament is opened to all willing to step into His loving grace and mercy through the power of the Gospel. Jesus has empowered all of us to live beyond the consequences of law. More specifically, above the law through the empowerment of righteousness and holiness. Grace empowers all of us to pursue Holiness and the Fruit of the Spirit. We must show our faith! Live our faith! Act upon our faith! But it can only come through being filled by God. Repentance is both asking forgiveness and turning from our sin. When we repent, we are emptying ourselves of sin and unrighteous living. It is the filling up of the Holy Spirit through the acceptance and blood of Jesus Christ. Quit following man's ways, or religious traditions, or placebo truths. Your only choice is to follow the real Jesus, who carries true power, real hope and eternal acceptance. Along with this get in a Bible-believing church where you can have daily opportunities to grow as well as have an extended family. Develop daily personal and corporate bible study, prayer and worship. Do not let pseudo-churches and pseudo-truths that are prevalent in our society mold you into *going* to church rather than *being* the church. Let the power of the grace of Jesus Christ transform us through filling us with righteousness and holiness. In the following chapters, we will discuss how to fight, overcome and defeat personal and societal devastations of the Bastard Curse.

Questions to ponder:

1. Give examples of how you have "come out of her?" What areas do you still need to work on?

2. Are you being the salt of the world? Why or Why Not?

3. What areas of your life do you want more of fix than a fixing?

4. Are there any areas of your life that give you almost constant pain? If so why haven't you done a one-eighty?

Chapter 7

Truths vs Pseudo Truths

(Lies)

WHAT IS TRUTH? JESUS SAID:

> John 14:6 Jesus said to him, "I am
> the Way, the Truth, and the Life; no
> one comes to the Father but by Me."

So, Jesus is the Truth! We live in a culture that likes relative truth - until your truth disagrees with mine and it irritates me. The liberal mindset I grew up under fought any type of censorship within the public schools. They cried out that children must have the opportunity to have viewpoints of the minority or from the side of socially unacceptable causes. These groups vigorously fought to keep books and other materials in the hands of children and others because of the freedom of speech and free press. This was truth to them. Now these same groups fight to censor Christian materials in the same settings. They wholeheartedly have become schizophrenic in their political beliefs. This proves that they were not out for the welfare of children and our society. They had an official agenda to push that was contrary to the social norm, and they used venomous threats to blast this agenda through. But now that they are in power they have become the fourth Reich. They talk tolerance but bully any ideas that disagree with them. Their view is that they are enlightened, and the rest of society must be whipped into alliance with their agenda. In their anything-goes truth, the only thing that has gone is Truth!

Even within the evolutionary truth they blindly follow, truth must have developed from something that contains and is truth. Cells came from cells. Truth cannot evolve from random pieces of information. Evolutionists cannot prove where truth comes from, therefore, truth must evolve. That means their truth is not Truth. It is only temporary truth, which, in my mind, is a lie. If someone chooses to rob a bank, because now it is their truth, we must let them according to "their" thinking. If a pedophile chooses to have sex with a minor, with or without their permission, it is okay because it is their truth. It doesn't matter if they hurt them or not. Someone must have randomly drawn a line in the sand to say, if you hurt someone then it is wrong. How about if that 50-year-old man makes that 5-year-old feel good. Then it must be okay, right? This putrid and disgusting way of thinking is becoming prevalent within our society. Our colleges and high schools are preaching to push the norms. "Fight the Man!" Except according to their own admissions, they represent the "state," better known as the "Man!" If that's the case, every teacher pushing their social-depravity agenda should expect their students to cheat, plagiarize, miss class and be mouthy. If their agenda of moral decay becomes the norm, then they must teach against it. But they won't.

As God pours His Spirit upon all flesh (Joel 2:28), we will continue to see a hunger increase for spiritual food. The problem is that the church continues to have a form of Godliness, but denies it power. Two forms of religion are increasing at an alarming rate: Islam and Witchcraft. Both are rooted in control and fear. They both offer power as well. See, as the church has been neutered to the reproduction of Christ within us, we don't offer any answer to the worlds emptiness and despair. People are already powerless and hopeless. Why would they run to Christians that are just as empty and powerless? So, they are settling for pseudo-spirituality.

Pseudo-spirituality is a false spirituality based upon the real spirituality of scripture. God's kingdom comes in power! When demons were cast out:

> Luke 10:9 And heal the sick that are in it, and say to them, The kingdom of God has come near you!

When we heal the sick through the power of Jesus Christ, we bring God's kingdom near them.

> Luke 11:20 But if I cast out demons with the finger of God, no doubt the kingdom of God has come on you.

If we cast out demons, we draw the Kingdom closer.

> Luke 12:31 But rather seek the kingdom of God, and all these things shall be added to you.

So, the associative property of algebra states that if A=B, and B=C, then A=C. If healing brings the kingdom, and casting out demons brings the kingdom, why don't we see it happen in the body of Christ? It's because we don't seek the kingdom. At least not His kingdom! We seek our own. So, if scripture is true, which it is, we lack in faith. We then lack in a Kingdom attitude. This leads us to building our own kingdom. We don't seek His kingdom or righteousness. We don't cast out demons, nor heal the sick. So, what's our purpose? What is our destiny? What are our consequences to these absences in our life? We will lack! We will lack peace, joy and love.

How many people do you know who are pseudo-happy? If they are "fake" in their walk, they will be fake in their "talk," and vice versa. Pseudo to me means fake. They wear a mask. Ever have fake friends? How did that make you feel? God doesn't want you to have the imitation. He wants you to have the authentic walk and talk. He wants you to have the real deal! Luke 12:32 states that it is His pleasure to give us His kingdom. After all, Thy Kingdom come, thy will be done. Are you doing His will?

> Acts 14:22 confirming the souls of the disciples, calling on them to continue in the faith and that through much tribulation we must enter into the kingdom of God.

If we do His kingdom calling, tribulation will come. We must be kingdom minded and driven by the heart of the King. We live in a culture of rebellion and disobedience. We hear it all the time. Don't tell me what to do, or I will rebel against it! Rules without relationship lead to rebellion. Rebellion is like the sin of Witchcraft. On the other hand, relationship without rules leads to lawlessness. In true Christianity, Jesus will never ever come to you and chastise you for being too obedient to the word. If Jesus is the word, and you disobey the word, you disobey Him. How can you willfully disobey Him and say we love Him? We cannot! Faith and obedience go hand in hand. Greasy grace quickly casts down a multitude of scripture. Many say, "none of the

Old Testament is for the Gentiles, and neither are some parts of the New Testament." We are again left with a "hole-e-bible." Except they have no problem claiming the promises of the Old Testament. If they believe what is said in the Old Testament scripture and verbiage, they are made under a different covenant. Why can't it be just one Testament of God's grace?

WHY NOT?

Questions to ponder:

1. When was the last time the Kingdom of God fell upon you?

2. When was the last time God poured Himself out through you to touch another person?

3. I have seen many miracles of deliverance throughout the last 20 years of ministering in this area. Truly the power of God's Kingdom shows up. Why do you think this is unpopular? Why don't more people work in this calling?

4. What does it take to enter into His Kingdom calling today?

Chapter 8

Step One: Submitted to

Jesus Christ

THE BEGINNING TO A NEW LIFE IN Christ is Christ himself. In Him there is life.

John 14:6 Jesus said to him, I am the Way, the Truth, and the Life; no one comes to the Father but by Me.

We have discussed, statistically, that the issues within the church mimic the issues outside the church. Why? Because we are in and of the world. We have allowed the church to be mixed with the world. Not only that but we have allowed the church to be molded into the world's ways. We cannot have two masters nor two creators. We will love one or the other, but always hate the opposite. A house divided will not stand! Besides, our God is a jealous God. He does not share equal status. God wants an intimate relationship with His bride, not a harlot!

> Ephesians 5:22 Wives, submit yourselves to your own husbands, as to the Lord.

If we are the bride, we are His wife and we are commanded to submit. Otherwise we are rebellious. Pride comes before the fall. Rebellion is like the sin of Witchcraft. So, in my mind and heart a lack of submission equals pride, Witchcraft, harlotry and prostitution. Even children are told to obey, which is a sign of obedience. Slaves obey your masters. Submission is a sign of humility. Humble yourself, or you will be humbled someday.

We must be sold out for Jesus. As one author put it: "My dignity for His deity." Lose yourself in Christ to find yourself in Christ. He must be our all-in-all. Holding back is to deny Him. Take your checkbook or calendar, and allow the leadership of your church to evaluate the focus of your time and money. How you spend your money or time clearly identifies what you leave room for, or worship and submit to.

We have a submission issue in our society. When I take the word apart we see: "Sub – Mission." Whatever we submit to, we become under (sub) their purpose (mission). The word defines what we become. We must submit to the will of the Father, spoken through Jesus, empowered through the Holy Spirit. We must submit to God.

> **James 4:7 Therefore submit your-selves to God. Resist the devil, and he will flee from you.**

We resist God, submit to the devil and we flee from God. The devil has been conquered and defeated and his works destroyed. But, we have been good at resurrecting the devil's schemes. His primary attacks focus on killing, stealing and destroying through the means of fear, doubt and lies. In hindsight, many in the church, if not most, deserve to be tormented or stolen from, not because of Jesus and His power, but, because not submitting to God means we have submitted to the other side.

Faith when activated causes us to draw closer to God. Faith exists anytime we can't go any further. Faith enacts submission. We must choose this day whom we will serve. Who do you serve? Yourself? Man? Mammon? We all place our "faith" into something. But, God has given each of us a measure of faith to respond to Him. Submission is a choice. Out of choice we move onward and upward. The more we humble ourselves the higher we go!

James 4:10 Be humbled before the Lord, and He will lift you up.

Quit hanging out with the turkeys in the barnyard when God has called you to soar with the eagles. Turkeys only fly when they can run no longer, and then only fly a short distance. Eagles soar (glide) for a long time on the wind (Holy Spirit). Their power comes from outside themselves. We are empowered through the Holy Spirit to do good works. More importantly, to do the greater works of Jesus Christ. Eagles must submit to the wind. We must submit to use His Holy Spirit's power.

Do you hunger and thirst after righteousness? To submit to a king means to love what He loves and hate what He hates. Submission is not on our terms. We won World War II, and Japan and Germany had to submit to the agreement of surrender for the battles to end. Maybe this is why we have so many internal struggles. We must surrender our lives over to the power and authority of Jesus Christ.

Questions to ponder:

1. Why is submitting a 'four letter' word to-day?

2. Are you submitted, one unto another?

3. Are you more of a turkey or an eagle? What would others say? Have someone interview them for you - I dare you!

4. Hungering and thirsting after righteousness is a lost art. We, more or less, will take it or leave it. What does submission have to do with this?

Chapter 9

Step Two: Empowered by Jesus Christ

SUBMISSION IS A NECESSARY foundational block of our faith. The question sometimes revolves around "if we can be born again without some form of submission to our Lord and Savior Jesus Christ." Can we ask for repentance without submission? We should struggle with submission, not in a negative, destructive way, but, rather in a constructive, soul-searching directive. After we submit, we must step into obedience. Not obedience in a have-to-earn-my-salvation way. Obedience is within relationship. We obey every word that proceeds from the mouth of God because of His position.

Many people obscure obedience by calling it legalism. Legalism is a heart issue, not an obedience issue. Many say God's laws have been done away with by Christ. But, Christ set the example by being obedient to His Father even unto death. If it was good enough for Him, why not us? This is where our western culture's rebellion comes in. We make up new rules that could easily turn into legalism.

I traveled to a conference in Minneapolis-Saint Paul a few years ago with two other men from our church. Unusual for me, we arrived early. As we walked around the church hosting the event, we met one of the greeters. He asked me where we were from. I said from northwestern Wisconsin, about two hours away. Then he asked from what church. I said Seventh Day Baptist. (Yes, a Baptist church who meets on the creational seventh day. The day God blessed and made Holy. We worship every day of the week, but follow the testimony of Jesus' obedience to His Father not out of salvation, but out of love.) Well, the man's countenance changed. He proceeded to aggressively attack us on the day we worship on ... which is legalistic!!! Wow! He didn't know us. He didn't even ask us why.

> Mark 3:35 For whoever does the will of God, the same is My brother and My sister and My mother.

When Christ came to the earth in the form of fully man and fully God, He didn't do away with the Law. He fulfilled the requirements of the Law which I could not fulfill. Since God doesn't change, His heart and character hasn't changed, nor ever will. The Father didn't go through anger management classes when His Son came to earth. And Jesus wasn't at the Heavenly Boarding School during the Old Testament. He is, was and will always be the Word! So, God's heart has not changed. Jesus was all over the Old Testament. Mercy and grace were evident in the Old Testament. In fact, I have a tough time breaking up scripture into two testaments. It is only ONE testament of our God! The Old Testament wasn't God's practice ground. He didn't get it wrong. His plan has always been the same. He has prepared the Way of reconciliation back to Him. The pathway is Genesis through the Revelation. It is fully Jesus Christ. Genesis through Revelation is the Word, and Jesus is the Word!

Because I am made in God's image and follow His creation design, what right do I have to set up rules for my children to follow if He has removed our rule. My relationship with my children is not based upon rules or laws. It is only helped to be preserved in good standing by staying away from consequences that will separate me from them. Our Father is no different. He created the Laws to be directives that describe His yearning for us not to be separated from Him. This is called sin. Sin is a four-letter word in our western culture of lawlessness. In fact, not teaching the whole Word for the last four decades has created a lawless society. Anything goes. Because of Jesus, God's laws can be written upon our hearts. Yet, a Godless society seems to be prevailing.

Yes, I know the Law was never intended to get us into heaven, anymore than any New Testament scripture. It is not the Bible that gets us into heaven. It is not going to church on Saturday or Sunday, or reading the Bible, or praying, or ministry, or good deeds, or tithing, or being baptized, or ... To say so would say would be legalistic and a perversion of His truth. The only way into heaven is to be a follower of Jesus Christ. When we do that we will do as He said in all of scripture. The Law, praying, baptism, church, miracles, spiritual gifts and Bible studies are all avenues to grow our relationship with the Father, Son and Holy Ghost. God has expectations of His children because He has expectations for Himself. He cannot deny Himself. He is love, kindness, hope, justice, peace and joy. He sustains these through Himself. To deny any part of His Word or character is to deny all of Him. Yes, it is true that if we break any part of God's Law we break it all and deserve damnation. The 'free' gift from God came through His Son (which wasn't free to Him because it cost Him everything). The Word says it's free to us, but also says it will cost us everything. It's kind of like being released from a zillion-dollar debt by giving the one who paid my bill a penny. What a transfer! I can't afford to pay off the debt. So, He pays it for me provided I also lay down my life for Him. I cannot earn salvation! I can only accept it and release it into my death to give me life.

Jesus within the scripture raised the bar for sin.

> Matthew 5:27-28 You have heard that it was said to the ancients, "You shall not commit adultery." But I say to you that whoever looks on a woman to lust after her has already committed adultery with her in his heart.

We no longer have to "do" the sin to commit it, we only have to "think" it. Not just a passing thought, but dwelling on it. This was probably His intent all along. But, before Jesus we were powerless for the most part to overcome sin. Grace is **not** the "big cover up," so people can sin more. It is also more than just unmerited favor. That is the beginning of grace, not the fullness of grace. Grace doesn't just forgive our sins because Jesus didn't just die for my sins. He rose from the dead. The Holy Spirit's power raised Him from the dead. The Holy Spirit's power doesn't want to just get you to forgiveness through Jesus Christ; the Holy Spirit wants to empower you. Lazarus was raised from the dead. You are to be raised from the dead. Jesus had Lazarus' grave clothes removed. We have too many Christians walking around in their grave clothes. They are wrapped up in the consequences of their pasts, demonic oppression, hurts and despair. The grave clothes restrict our movement and life. We ARE empowered to be over-comers. We are more than conquerors!

> Romans 8:37 But in all these things we more than conquer through Him who loved us.

It comes down to obedience. We must be obedient to God's grace. Period! Jesus was sacrificed for our sins. He rose again to promise us a resurrection and an empowered life. Jesus prepared us for victory and freedom. We will not be sinless on this side of eternity, but we should be transformed into sinning less each day. We are to become more like Christ each day. To deny this is to deny the power of the resurrection and its transformational grace.

The key to our walk is Jesus' authority and power. If we look in Genesis, Jesus delegated authority to Adam and Eve to go into all the world.

> Genesis 1:28 And God blessed them. And God said to them, Be fruitful, and multiply and fill the earth, and subdue it. And have dominion over the fish of the sea and over the fowl of the heavens, and all animals that move upon the earth.

God's plan for man was to conquer. God had the power, but delegated His authority over to man. Subduing and dominion are both authority terms. God's plan was for the earth to be stewarded by mankind. Yet, the only earthly substance reserved for Him was the tree of the knowledge of good and evil. He did not want His creational likeness to partake in even the knowledge of evil. Yet, we still choose to know evil. I still hear people say that it is better that they learn through their own mistakes. They want to taste sin. Wow! The same sin that got us in trouble in the garden still gets us in trouble today. God calls us into holiness, not holes in life. God deigned us into obedience, not rebellion. Rebellion is like the sin of Witchcraft (1 Samuel 15:23). Jesus restored our role when He won back the authority by death, burial and resurrection; that's why He could say to "US" the following scriptural orders.

> Matthew 28:19 Therefore go and teach all nations, baptizing them in the name of the Father and of the Son and of the Holy Spirit,

> Matthew 28:20 teaching them to observe all things, whatever I commanded you. And, behold, I am with you all the days until the end of the world. Amen.

or

Mark 16:15-18 And He said to them,
Go into all the world, proclaim the
gospel to all the creation. He who
believes and is baptized will be saved,
but he who does not believe will be
condemned. And miraculous signs
will follow to those believing these
things: in My name, they will cast out
demons; they will speak new tongues;
they will take up serpents; and if
they drink any deadly thing, it will not
hurt them. They will lay hands on the
sick, and they will be well.

Both in Genesis and in the end of Matthew and Mark, we see God telling us to subdue creation. Since the fall creation has been ruling us. Remember the threat of animals that eat us or have a venom. Remember the plants that can poison us. Therefore, we have addictions to things like marijuana, cocaine, and other "natural herbs which now destroy lives, families and society. The argument is that "God made them", so therefore He put them here for us to get high on. Except, they begin to rule over our mind, will and emotions! We are under the control of the creation!

Genesis 1:29 And God said, Behold!
I have given you every herb seeding
seed which is upon the face of all the
earth, and every tree in which is the
fruit of a tree seeding seed; to you it
shall be for food.

The herbs were to be food for us. They were to be sustenance and health for our bodies.

> Psalms 104:14 He causes the grass
> to grow for the cattle, and plants for
> the service of man, to bring forth
> food out of the earth,

> Psalms 104:15 and wine cheers the
> heart of man, and oil makes his face
> shine, and bread sustains the heart
> of man.

But, man traded ruler ship for slavery, addictions and torment. If God is not in control of your life, then something else probably controlling you. It's time for us to commit our ways to the Lord. Don't surround yourself with God, but place Him at the center of everything you do. Remember, we should be walking in victory and fullness. But, most people walk in defeat an emptiness.

A spirit of control is evident in our culture and within our churches. Witchcraft is a spirit of control. Witchcraft, wiccans and druids worship the creation rather than the Creator. It is true that I am seeing more and more Witchcraft entering the church through drugs, alcohol, video games, movies, tattoos, piercings and control. Many Christians are turning to "new age" treatments like Yoga, transcendental meditation and acupuncture, instead of turning to God's miraculous methods. One well-known doctor states the medical field does not know the cause of about 80 percent of all diseases. It is my belief that because the body of Christ has left their first love, Jesus, we fall from beneath His protective umbrella. We will continue to be destroyed by new, extreme diseases. Cancer rates will continue to escalate. Contrary to popular belief, which blames genetically modified foods and other secular reasoning's, it is an absence of God in our lives that will be our demise. I have been doing many more deliverances on Christians who have a spirit of Witchcraft in them. It is not pretty to see them come out. It is humbling to see demonic activity torment and make the impotent when it comes to salvations and transformations. Yes, Jesus name and blood is still casting out demons, healing, giving signs and wonders, dreams and visions. Even in a Baptist boy like me!

I am excited to watch God use a man like me. As Pastor Barry Baugh, a friend, says: "I am a nobody that came to tell everybody about somebody who can save anybody." My call is to develop modern-day Nazarites, ones who are truly separate from the world. But, engage it where people are at. We must develop people who are in the world, but not of it. Most of the church does exactly what the world does, thinking it is connecting to people. They are connecting to people, by creating unhealthy soul ties. We are NOT doing what we were told:

Revelation 18:4 And I heard another voice from Heaven, saying, Come out of her, My people, that you may not be partakers of her sins, and that you may not receive of her plagues.

The world's pattern is like Babylon. We must come out of her and be separate. We must be that counter-culture. Instead we talk, dress, eat, drink and divorce like the world. In fact, we equal or surpass the world in many statistical issues of the day. We still miss the purpose of Jesus Christ. Most still ask what can I do and still be saved. We should be asking Jesus "do You want us to flee from even the appearance of evil?" Maybe if the Bible doesn't clearly state we should do it, we should refrain from it. The above verse shows that God's people will receive the same plagues as the world does. Is the church receiving these plagues? Absolutely and even higher. All the sins of the world are beginning to be accepted. We WILL receive the same plagues, and the same consequences. Some of these are hopelessness, despair, low self-esteem, hatred, suicide, sexual sins, addictions, paranoia, anxiety, depression, multiple personalities, sickness and disease, and many more! We are reaping the same consequences, because the church is not set apart; it is partaking fully of the world. Our children are paying for it, and our communities are okay with it. Shame on us. Shame comes from the evil one. We are being destroyed. Where is the humble, the holy, the righteous, the loving, the prayers, the servants, the ...

> Hosea 4:6 My people are destroyed for lack of knowledge. Because you have rejected knowledge, I will also reject you from being priest to Me. Since you have forgotten the Law of your God, I will also forget your sons, even I.

We are being destroyed because we lack knowledge, or better yet refuse Truth. We have denied whole sections of the scripture and wonder why we are being destroyed. Duh! We have lost whole generations of the next leaders because we have lost His precepts (Laws), His ways, His Heart! We have some coming back, but mostly to a powerless gospel of a "sugar daddy" or the "God-father".

Jesus has the power (dunamis)and authority (exousia). He has delegated them for us to use through the Holy Spirit. We are to know Him, not just know about Him. Even demons know about Him and shudder. We aren't that wise! We are to be more supernatural than natural. Our spirits are to be bigger than our soul or flesh. But I guess if we don't feed it, it will atrophy. Our flesh and souls will grow and thicken. This will encapsulate our spirit which is where the Holy Spirit speaks to and through.

Questions to ponder:

1. Why do you feel it is easy for people to iden-
   tify with Jesus even when they don't think
   he was the messiah or even God?

2. Is following Jesus the end all, or did He have
   more for us?

3. What part of the creation has you in bondage? What are the fruits of this bondage?

4. Do you walk in His power and authority?
   What are your fruits of doing so?

Chapter 10

Step Three: Empowered

by the Holy Spirit

JESUS BOUGHT OUR VICTORY WITH His death, burial and resurrection. Yet, we remain divided and conquered. We sing a multitude of songs and hymns that lift the name of Jesus on high, and the body of Christ slips deeper and deeper into shame, guilt and despair. Hopelessness, sinfulness and selfishness abound within the walls of our churches because it fills the cavity of our hearts. We can reproduce only what we are, not what we hope to be. This is because we have not received the fullness of the Gospel. We may have Jesus, because we can understand laying down our lives for someone we love, but, we don't embrace the Holy Spirit, the Holy Ghost. Even the disciples waited in the upper room for the "power" to show up. Maybe it's because we have money, abilities and goals that we rely upon ourselves rather than relying upon Him. Do you yearn for the presence of the Holy Spirit? Unlike Jesus, He does not make sense.

Scripture says:

> **1 Corinthians 2:10 But God has revealed them to us by His Spirit; for the Spirit searches all things, yea, the deep things of God.**

No one understands the fullness of God, especially the deep things of God. The Holy Spirit does this and reveals this to us in due time. The Holy Spirit must be the vessel by which we read scripture, dreams, revelation, Truth and peace. The good, bad and the ugly can be revealed by the Holy Spirit. Nothing can be hidden from the Holy Spirit.

> **Daniel 2:22 He reveals the deep and secret things; He knows what is in the darkness, and the light dwells with Him.**

He is the part of the Trinity that empowers sanctification. Jesus justifies us. The Holy Spirit sanctifies us. Scripture states that:

> 2 Thessalonians 2:13 But we are bound to give thanks always to God for you, brothers beloved of the Lord, because God has from the beginning chosen you to salvation through sanctification of the Spirit and belief of the truth,

and

> Hebrews 12:14 Follow peace with all, and holiness, without which no one shall see the Lord;

The word for "holiness" is *hagiasmos (hag-ee-as-mos')*. *This is defined as purification*, that is, (the state) *purity*; concretely (by Hebraism) a *purifier:* - holiness, sanctification. Could we say that without sanctification no one will see the Lord? Justification isn't enough. The two work in harmony and unity together. It appears that this is a process of grace.

> 2 Corinthians 8:6 for us to call on Titus, that even as he began before, so he would also complete this grace to you also.

The major problems in the modern western church is either a lack of the Holy Spirit, or a prostituting of Him. We ignore Him by "us" being in control of the services and our lives. We also tend to make Him a "bells and whistle" show. His main purpose is to draw us closer to both the Father and our Savior. He empowers us.

No wonder the church has a greasy grace and wishy-washy ways. We have lost our passion and focus because we have lost the one entrusted with the power and heart to implant into us. We talk about "it," and some even talk about Him. But, how many of us rely upon Him! Not upon our Greek, Hebrew, apologetics and hermeneutics.

The Father sent Jesus who sent the Holy Spirit (Ghost). The way to the Father is through the Son who is found through the Holy Spirit. We cannot find the true Jesus without the Holy Spirit, and we cannot find the Father without the Spirit leading us to Christ who leads us to the Father. Is it any wonder why the church is dead and flat-lined, because its "heart" is absent of the Holy Spirit? Jesus was full of the Holy Spirit.

> Luke 4:1 And Jesus, full of the Holy Spirit, returned from Jordan and was led by the Spirit into the wilderness

Another scripture is stronger in the Holy Spirit's role.

> Mark 1:12-13 And immediately the Spirit drove Him into the wilderness. And He was there in the wilderness forty days, tempted by Satan. And He was with the wild beasts, and the angels ministered to Him.

The Spirit "drove" Jesus into the desert to be tempted, or better yet to be strengthened for our example. Yet, angels ministered to Him there also. God, in the midst of our temptations and struggles, wants to minister to us, sometimes even through angels. Could you withstand a '40-day' desert experience? You could if you were "full" of the Spirit!

Jesus needed to be full of the Holy Spirit to overcome the temptation in the wilderness. It is ironic that many of the splendid examples in scripture were rooted in the wilderness experiences: Jesus, John the Baptist, Moses, Joshua and David. These men were tested and formed in the wilderness. Just look at the pinnacle example of Jesus. He was tempted in the lust of the eyes, the lust of the flesh and the pride of life. These three areas are where we are tempted. We will fail if we are not growing deeper into submission with the Holy Spirit. God does not tempt us, but He will lead us through the temptation of the enemy to victory. But if we fail the temptation, we will wander the desert.

Many Christians are there now. They've accepted Christ as their Savior, but lack total surrender to the Holy Spirit to lead them into God's goodness. They hang on to the pain and habits of their past which will bring only more torment, because now they have a war waging within them.

> Hebrews 3:7-9 Therefore, as the Holy Spirit says, "Today if you will hear His voice, do not harden your hearts, as in the provocation, in the day of temptation in the wilderness, when your fathers tempted Me, proved Me, and saw My works forty years.

Temptation happens in the wilderness. We have the opportunity to become better or bitter. We become bold or begin to grow spiritual mold. Here it says we will harden our hearts when we fail to the temptation. But if we persevere we become stronger and vibrant. The length of your wilderness is set by God. You cannot shorten it, but may extend it because of your attitude and faithlessness.

> Hebrews 3:17 But with whom was He grieved forty years? Was it not with those who had sinned, whose carcasses fell in the wilderness?

> John 6:49 Your fathers ate the manna in the wilderness, and died.

Even though God sustained them in their disobedience, they still died. Their manna fed them. (Maybe they had 101 Ways to Prepare Manna Cookbook, or maybe not.) Their shoes didn't wear out. The wilderness wasn't the intended destination. But because of Egypt still being in their hearts, He had to remove it via the desert (wilderness). Many, maybe most of the Body of Christ are the same way. The wilderness times are prepared for us to get the world's ways out of us (sanctification and transformation). Grieve the Holy Spirit's work in you, and see how you feel and act.

> Isaiah 32:15 until the Spirit is poured on us from on high, and the wilderness becomes a fruitful field, and the fruitful field is thought to be a forest.

God wants our wilderness experiences to be transformed into fruitful fields. Fruit brings refreshment, nourishment and beauty. The fruit of the Spirit is: love, joy, peace, longsuffering, kindness, goodness, faith, meekness, self-control (against such things there is no law) (Gal 5:22-23). Fruit is also what we produce or reproduce in life. God has placed inside of us His seed to reproduce it in others. Are you and I producing and reproducing these attributes in our lives and others?

> *Isaiah 32:16 Then judgment shall dwell in the wilderness, and righteousness remain in the fruitful field.*

God makes a judgment in the wilderness. Do you repeat the temptation because you gave up or caved in? Or do you have the wilderness transform into a fruitful field? Passing through the wilderness develops character. Character in God is righteousness. So many people think God is out to get them, when really, He has a plan to get them out!

There is a second type of wilderness. Sometimes the wilderness is a place for us to meet with God and receive wisdom and fresh revelation of who He is and His plan for our lives. In the last days, the "woman" will have to retreat to the wilderness for a time. John the Baptist lived in the wilderness. In these cases, the wilderness is prepared by God as a refuge and restoration. It is probably for the ones who already conquered the temptation wilderness. Do you think this might be the reason why so many can't find peace and content-ment in the body of Christ? They stay in the temptation wilderness and keep repeating its struggles. Again, the wilderness is a place to be purified and solidified in Christ. When we are not holy, its role is to make us holy. After we are holy, the wilderness is a place where we find our refuge in God.

> Revelation 12:6 And the woman fled into the wilderness, where she had a place prepared by God, so that they might nourish her there a thousand, two hundred and sixty days.

> Revelation 12:14 And two wings of a great eagle were given to the woman, so that she might fly into the wilder-ness, into her place, where she is nourished for a time and times and half a time, from the serpent's face.

We are loved by a jealous God who wants us for Himself and for His children to eat only from the tree of life (Jesus). As mentioned before, to see the Father we must enter through the Son by which we get to through the Holy Spirit. Jesus still is Immanuel (God with Us) but through the Holy Spirit. By the below verses we can see an important Truth sandwiched between two easy to swallow promises. The Truth between them holds the two together. If we fail to follow the middle one the other two are disqualified. We must come out of the world. After all, we are citizens of a different system/kingdom not of this world. To love this world means the Father's love is not in us (1 John 2:15). In fact, James 4:4 says to be a friend with the world is to be an enemy of God.

> 2 Corinthians 6:16-18 And what agreement does a temple of God *have* with idols? For you are the temple of *the* living God, as God has said, "I will dwell in them and walk among *them*; and I will be their God, and they shall be My people." Therefore, come out from among them and be separated, says the Lord, and do not touch the unclean *thing*. And I will receive you and I will be a Father to you, and you shall be My sons and daughters, says *the* Lord Almighty.

So how do we do it? It is done by the Holy Spirit's power. Our job is to die so we may live. Problem is that most people don't really know what the "life, and life more abundant" that Christ promises us, really looks and feels like. If we did, we wouldn't be complaining and lying dormant in our faith. We would be enacting our faith unto righteousness. We would be overflowing in God. Some of the fruit of having faith is that signs and wonders would follow those who believe. Bible studies and prayer times would be packed out. Services would be standing room only. Individuals would not be able to contain the Good News. Evangelism would be natural and an everyday occurrence. Salvations and deliverances would be expected routinely. Prayers of healing and miracles would be shouting the Truth of Jesus throughout the land. We would actually be living out the purpose and examples Christ gave us to be.

> Galatians 5:24-25 But those belonging to Christ have crucified the flesh with its passions and lusts. If we live in the Spirit, let us also walk in the Spirit.

But how many of us have crucified all the flesh with its passion and lusts? We can either focus on the flesh or be led by the Spirit. Jesus was led by the Spirit. He could do only what the father was doing and His will dictated. He knew this because the Spirit searches the heart of God. Jesus needed this because He was limited in His earthly "body". We too are limited. That is why we must be totally and utterly dependent upon the leading of the Holy Spirit. To be Christ's we must crucify the flesh. See we are either owned by the devil, or we have turned over ownership to Christ. We are either for Him or against Him. There is no gray area here. So where do you stand?

Maybe I'm wrong. Maybe only Jesus was full of the Holy Spirit. Or maybe everybody is full of the Holy Spirit when they come to Christ. Let us look at some scriptures.

> Acts 6:3 Therefore, brothers, look out among you seven men being witnessed to, full of the Holy Spirit and wisdom, whom we may appoint over this duty.

Acts 6:5 And the saying pleased
all the multitude. And they chose
Stephen, a man full of faith and
of the Holy Spirit, and Philip, and
Prochorus, and Nicanor, and Timon,
and Parmenas, and Nicholas, a pros-
elyte of Antioch.

Acts 7:55 But being full of the
Holy Spirit, looking up intently into
Heaven, he saw the glory of God, and
Jesus standing at the right hand of
God.

Acts 11:24 For he was a good man
and full of the Holy Spirit and faith.
And many people were added to the
Lord.

The examples above have them searching within
the body of believers for people "full" of the Spirit.
This was a bar being set. Evidently not everyone was
full of the Spirit. There was and still is differing levels
of infiltration of the Holy Spirit based upon brokenness
and submission to Him. Also, in the examples above
we see specifics of those full of the Spirit. They were
to witness the fullness of the Spirit. Do we even know
what the fullness looks like? Most Christians are fuller
of themselves than of the Holy Spirit. The church has
traded the fullness of the Holy Spirit to people who
are talented in organization and church programming.
Remember, we are evangelizing here in America only
one percent of the population. Most churches are in de-

cline. Most churches that are increasing do so because of the shuffling of "sheep". Very few conversions into disciples. Most just make converts that lack transformation and power in their lives. It is written in 2 Timothy 3:5 that in the last days man will have a form of godliness but deny its power. Jesus Christ did not die so I could remain the same. In my "death" I will live by the transforming power released through the Holy Spirit. We are living in the last days. Again, I say, men and women go to church, but lack the power to become the church because they deny His power through the Holy Spirit. Church is a hang-out time with very little covenant and knowing those that labor among you. Church, especially in America, still remains a place of entertainment and social acceptance. While we are to bless people, the church has become a social distribution center much like Hollywood. Works alone will not get people to heaven, just like faith won't. We preach the gospel in word and deeds.

I believe more attention should be placed upon the deeds that Jesus did, and be empowered to do them daily. Healing, deliverance, miracles and the like are solely rooted in Christ. It is very hard to steal a testimony away from someone who just got healed of cancer, or sight given back, or hearing, or delivered from demons they didn't even know they had or didn't even believe in. Man cannot imitate these deeds like they can by feeding the poor or helping the homeless.

I am not advocating stopping these, but we can generally accomplish these missions in our own abilities. Healing, deliverance and miracles need the total and complete surrendering to the Holy Spirit. But again, man offsets his lack of being led by the Holy Spirit by doing more stuff that all men can do, regardless if they are saved of not. My expectation is that God will do more abundantly than what I could ever ask for or dream of. We see Jesus doing these things at the heart of His ministry, and then teaching His disciples to do the same, and for them to teach it to as many that are as far off ... US! The Holy Spirit empowered Jesus, He empowered the Disciples and their disciples, AND He empowers US! Just something to think about.

What is Jesus' and the Father's emphasis/weightiness placed upon the Holy Spirit?

> Matthew 12:31 Therefore I say to you, All kinds of sin and blasphemy shall be forgiven to men, but the blasphemy against the Holy Spirit shall not be forgiven to men.

If we are blasphemous towards the Spirit and His position and purpose, we will not be forgiven. I personally feel this means our hearts will become hard, because He is the One who draws us to the Son unto the Father. The hard part for me is that the Holy Spirit is the most difficult of the Trinity to place in a box to control Him. Our society doesn't like it when we can't explain a situation. But again, can any of us fathom the fullness of God in our earthly bodies? I think not.

I heard it put recently that our faith is like a puzzle. As most of us, we put together the border then fill in the middle. God's character represented within scripture is like the border of our faith. Everything God does in our lives does not violate the Truth of this border. But, many applications of this Truth look different than it might have 2000 years ago. Yet, it will not contradict God's Word found in scripture (the border). When we leave out pieces of the puzzle (God's Truth) we leave a foothold for the enemy to come and attack. He may even take up residence in our life. We can still be owned by God, but tormented by the enemy. In fact, most Christians I have found are tormented, not just tempted. They love the world. They are friends of the world while trying to be Christians.

Bastard children need to be surrounded by the fullness of the Holy Spirit. It is the Spirit who draws them and can transform their lives. Illegitimate children need a family to be adopted into. Since we all have been adopted back to God, what better place than the church. But the church will have to change. The American church family meets once or twice a week. Most people travel farther than they should. They aren't effectively ministering the Gospel to their area. Families far apart find it hard to keep fostering current relationships let alone developing new ones.

Illegitimate children are created in these long-distance relationships, many times outside the Biblical covenant a "family" needs. We are trying to raise spiritual children in spiritual orphanages or spiritual boarding schools. We all know how well most orphanages and boarding schools do. We are called to know those who labor among us. We are called to carry one another's burdens. We are called to lay hands on those who are sick and they will get well. I don't think God wanted that limited to one or two days a week, or to just 5-15 people in our church. Many say this can't be done in our culture where people come and go, and miss church 50 percent of the time. Sports and schools are demanding that our children be there. Well, maybe we should quit letting culture determine our church, and start letting a holy and powerful God show up at the church service and redeem our culture. Let us quit recycling the sheep through our doors, and start bringing in new sheep that were just transformed from being goats, or maybe even wolves.

The evil one enters in through worldly lust and desires and steals, kills and destroys the pieces of the puzzle God intended for us to use to get the picture. Most, I believe will not attain the "fullness" of what God intended because of our cravings for worldly "food". While they may still be saved, they lack the fullness of the Spirit living inside them. Many times, they feel empty or don't feel God's presence (which we don't need to feel God, but I know it sure helps me when I am struggling in my own life). His whole plan is to reveal it to us. But we must seek after Him to find it. We must search it out.

> **Proverbs 25:2 The glory of God is to hide a thing; but the honor of kings is to search out a matter.**

I believe God reveals His secrets and plans to those He can trust. Are you one He can trust? But, don't expect God to reveal His applications of the unseen until you are becoming more faithful in the seen, the Word of God! If we are faithful in the little He will give us much! We need to overflow in God through the indwelling of the Holy Spirit. We do this by submitting, surrendering, seeking and soaking up His presence and Truth. Then watch out! He commanded us to pray without ceasing, because He wants to communicate with His beloved. Not the harlot (slut) that is fornicating with the world or the adulterous bride cheating on her Groom. He is jealous. He is Holy seeking after a Holy bride. It is the role of the Holy Spirit to impart His Holiness upon the bride. It is His role to prepare the bride for her Groom, much like Esther had to before she married the King. It was about a year of bathing in fragrances to remove the junk of the world. We are to bath in the fragrances of the Holy Spirit's anointing. Are we preparing ourselves to meet our King? Are you stinking of the world, or are you putting off those things and putting on the aroma of the Holy

Spirit? You may fool the noses of those around you some of the time, but God has perfect smelling ability. He knows your "smell"! Is it a fragrance or a stench?

Questions to ponder:

1. Have you stopped at the justification of Jesus and refused the sanctification that the Spirit does? In other words, did you say the "magic words" to ask Jesus into your heart, and then continued on with your former lifestyle?

2. How big of a box have you placed the Holy Spirit in?

3. Jesus didn't die so you could fail in the flesh to the temptations of chasing after the world. So what temptations do you feed on that mimic the world?

4. Most Christians because of their own desires mock obedience as legalism. Yet, obedience to God's will and word release the Holy Spirit's power and miracles. Are you walking in the power and miraculous? Why or why not? What's holding you back?

Chapter 11

Step Four: Power

of Spiritual Warfare

So, **WHETHER YOU ARE AN ACTUAL** illegitimate child or a spiritually illegitimate one, the consequences are the same. Both deal with insecurity and low esteem, and both have hard times stepping into covenant relationships like marriages and church memberships. Both run from place to place looking for a place to fit in but never find peace or rest. No matter how hard they try or how many times they re-plant themselves into a new "soil," the end results are the same. Symptoms include depression, cutting, drugs/alcohol, sexual sins, rejection, abandonment and condemnation. We can eradicate most of these "symptoms" by eradicating the bastard child - both the physical and spiritual ones. As mentioned earlier, we have a culture of hurt and abused people. Not just physically or emotionally, but even deeper at the root of who we are, the spirit. Who we are is rooted in the spirit of man. Just as eternity is placed in the heart of man, so is our identity. Our bodies change, our minds change, but God breaths his Spirit into man. The identity of man can be found only in the identity of God. Because God is eternal and never changing, He is the only gauge we can really upon. If our identity is within anything else, we would be in constant flux. In fact, most people struggle with their identity. They place it in things that can be taken away and stolen from us.

Bastard (Illegitimate) children really struggle with their identity. In meeting and counseling people of all ages it is usually obvious by their symptoms that they were formed outside a covenant marriage. They are children carrying a curse placed upon them by their parents. A curse that allows the devil to discourage, torment and pour the guilt, shame and condemnation all over their life. As a society we can only reproduce what we are: ILLEGITIMACY!

By the blood of Jesus Christ and the empowerment of the Holy Spirit we can break this curse, and acquire the new DNA of Jesus Christ so we can look more like our Daddy in Heaven. It is really powerful when the parents who placed this curse upon their

children repent. Repentance stops the curse from progressing. Then a new path can be acquired through loosing God's provision into the child no matter what the age. We then command the enemy to leave in the name of Jesus, go to the dry place and not to return. This doesn't mean they will never come knocking in times of struggle wanting back in. But if we cleaned our house with the blood of Jesus Christ, and filled it up with the presence and power of the Holy Spirit, it will not have room to sneak in.

If in doubt or fear, you can ask a team of Spirit-filled believers to assist you in your deliverance from this curse. Your whole life and future will begin to blossom. We live in a culture that walks in illegitimacy and the garbage that goes with it. People are fearful of relationship and intimacy, but perfect love casts out the fear, and intimacy replaces the illegitimacy. People will crave deeper relationship with God, and those in His family. Scriptures states that:

> Psalms 1:1-3 Blessed is the man who has not walked in the counsel of the ungodly, and has not stood in the way of sinners, and has not sat in the seat of the scornful. But his delight is only in the Law of Jehovah; and in His Law he meditates day and night. And he shall be like a tree planted by the rivulets of water that brings forth its fruit in its seasons, and its leaf shall not wither, and all which he does shall be blessed.

The world gives us wicked counsel. Sinners give us wicked counsel. By the world's standards, fornication (sex outside the covenant of marriage) is accepted and encouraged. However, the break up rate is 50 percent higher than the average divorce rate in these fornicating relationships. Yet, divorce is now the norm. Divorce brings on hate, anger, paranoia and insecurities, in the adults and even greater consequences of suicide, drug and alcohol use, a greater number of sexual partners and corresponding STDs/STIs in the children. So why do most do it? Because that is what they've been taught, and there are demonic spirits lying and tormenting them into going deeper and deeper into their own pain. Pain has become the norm, and is expected. Any time we sin, it opens the door for the enemy to attack us and our families. Yet, our communities are okay with losing a child here and there to drugs, alcohol, suicide, depression and gangs. In fact, we expect and almost encourage our children to rebel against us and God.

> 1 Samuel 15:23 For rebellion is as the sin of Witchcraft, and stubbornness is as iniquity and idol worship. Because you have rejected the Word of Jehovah, He has also rejected you from being king!

Is it any wonder that the religion of Witchcraft is one of the fastest growing religions in our culture? We have traded the truths of God's Word for the lies of the world. We have pushed our children into Witchcraft and its devastation. We are called to rule as kings in this world, but, because of the fall, the creation now rules over us. What a difference from when God allowed man to name all the creatures. (Naming something is a sign of authority. Who named your children?) What a difference from God telling Adam to go into all the earth and subdue it, and to keep it under your authority? We have been rejected as rulers. Jesus restored our position in the commission when He said "Go into all the earth preaching ..." Sinners are stilled ruled by the creation. Look at pot or cocaine or cigarettes or alcohol or ... These created substances now rule the hearts and bodies of people. Lust and pride are spiritual cancers destroying the lives of those not redeemed from the curse through the deliverance (salvation) of Jesus Christ.

It should not be that the things of the world should rule over His people who are called to be kings and ambassadors carrying His authority. Christians should not be struggling with the same things as sinners. They might start out with them, but we should be shedding them by the power of Jesus Christ through the release of the Holy Spirit.

Obedience is a lost art as well. We have a culture of a weak church that is being conquered by the same sins the world is. So, it's easier to make an excuse for your sin than it is to die to your selfish desires and to kill them! It seems like most come to Christ for that fire insurance they are going to need when they get done playing and indulging in all the flaming sinful attitudes and lifestyles. This is not scriptural. Without Holiness (sanctification) no one will see the Lord (Hebrews 12:14). God commands us to be Holy. It must be a choice then. A choice to walk in it. A choice to put on Christ. He died so we can live out in obedience what He commands us to do. All these things are spiritual battles: how we live, what we watch, what we do to our bodies, what we think, what we listen to. The list goes on. We must examine our thoughts and actions and ask ourselves this question: does this draw me closer to God or away from Him? There is not much gray area really.

Obedience keeps the door of hearts closed to any type of spiritual intruder. God did not give us any of the commandments to be mean or anti-fun. He knows what is good and bad for us. The artist has the right to determine the purpose of the masterpiece. So He does with us. But we listen to the one who lies, cheats, steals and destroys. People get weirded out when I perform a deliverance ministry, or even talk about it. They make the devil omnipotent and God-like in his qualities. He does have power, but very limited. After all, he was created like us, or even a pebble. He gets only what God has allowed him to do. In the act of spiritual warfare, it is our role to either allow or restrict access to our lives through obedience or disobedience. The world is placing its hand on the hot stove of sin and is asking for an aspirin to take its pain away. However, God is calling them to remove their hand and heal will heal every wound or blister in their lives.

But again, the problem remains the same. The world is so used to the pain and suffering of being away from Christ, that it thinks it is normal. Even more alarming is that most people in the church think the same thing. We will always struggle in this world. That is true! But most are struggling to keep their head above water. Above the water in a toilet that is being flushed along with all the other waste. (I was careful in my verbiage.) People carrying the consequences of illegitimacy need to have the power of Jesus revealed through the Holy Spirit to free them from the "flush" of the world.

> *John 8:36 Therefore if the Son shall make you free, you shall be free indeed.*

We will not find freedom in any religious activity, only a power experience with Jesus Christ and the Holy Spirit. All Christians need to have a daily power experience with them both. That lets us know they are God and we are not. This reminds us of where true power and authority comes from and how we need to be tapped into them.

The churches are in dire need of true power experiences with God. I believe this is why the people who come from what we would call the deepest and darkest sins, seem to get on fire for God. They become radical in a ridiculous world. I've had some, older in their faith, state that in time those people will moderate in their zeal and become more likeable.

Recently, I was talking to a young man in our community that stated that people in my church were nicer to talk to because they weren't so "God crazy." He meant it as a compliment, but my spirit was immediately convicted! We had lost our saltiness, our flavor. We began to taste like the world, and the world could handle it. I am not for weirdness for the sake of weirdness. But, I am for the Jesus weirdness where He healed the sick, raised the dead, gave sight to the blind, hearing to the deaf, did miracles. Then He empowered all His disciples to do the same through the Holy Spirit. If we ONLY do these things, I'm sure the world won't think we're weird at all.

You want to break free of the "stinkin' thinkin'" in your life? Then make a break for the One who can do more than you could ever dream or imagine: Jesus Christ! Receive His Holy Spirit in His fullness. Quit chasing after entertainment both in and out of the church! Quit going to church for only one to two hours a week. If you can't hang with your church family throughout the week, you're probably not doing church Biblically. Small churches have failed, mega churches are failing. American churches need to become Biblical seven days a week. They don't need to become social institutions or welfare dispensers. The church needs to preach Jesus, preach repentance, live Jesus, live repented lives, lives full of Holy Ghost power. Everything else we do is secondary to the work of Jesus Christ and the Holy Spirit. Jesus came to liberate the captive (not through programming) heal the hurting (not through the world's medical system) and release hope (not through drugs and relationships) to everyone through one name only - Jesus Christ. The Holy Spirit is representing Jesus while He is in heaven with the Father. You should be representing Him too!

Questions to ponder:

1. Children must be conceived and born within the covenant of marriage to eradicate the bastard child. Why do people choose to destroy their future families by believing the lies of our sex-crazed society? It is almost like society will sacrifice the loss of the children to satisfy the lusts of the flesh.

2. Spiritual children must also be "born" through the relationship of the church. Yet, our current churches exploit the "relationless faith" where people go to a church only once a week and progress meaningless entertainment of chills and thrills to the masses. Do you go to church or are you an Acts church member that meets daily with the church for edifying and empowering?

3. Mediocrity is an epidemic in our society. Yet, when someone is radically changed by the power of Christ released through the Holy Spirit, society wants that person to have a lukewarm faith. But, not when it comes to sports, dating relationships and work. Are

you more radical for Jesus or for the things of this world? Remember we could always pull out your checkbook ledger or planner and see how and where you spend your time!

4. Do you want the pain to be dulled in life or do you want a different lifestyle that removes the choices that results in the painful consequences? A wise man once taught me that, if you remove the garbage the rats will go away. Most people want the fun garbage of life, and wonder where all the consequential rats came from.

Chapter 12

Keeping out of the Ditches

of Lawlessness and

Legalism

So where does all this leave us? People live in the ditches of life. They try to follow God through legalism or lawlessness. Legalism replaces relationship with rules. Lawlessness replaces relationship with selfishness. Relationship with God in Christ through the Holy Spirit requires a set of standards to live by and freedom to grow the relationship within the bounds of the covenant that God provides His protection. It has been said that there are more commandments "to do" in the New Testament than in the Old Testament.

Some claim there are over 600! It takes empowerment of the Holy Spirit to live within the bounds of freedom that Christ provides within His covenant. Holiness is demanded of us. Love is demanded of us. Outside His "covenantal" boundaries, He disciplines and the world destroys. Both occur simultaneously. We have a to do list. We have been called, equipped and empowered by Him. Yet, we choose to live as orphans, as illegitimates, as bastard children in the church and in the world.

To stay out of these ditches, we need to partake of individual and corporate worship. I'm not talking about just music. That is what the church already is doing as we discussed earlier. Worship begins following the four steps we just discussed. It is our whole life. Our families, our jobs, our homes, our thoughts, our desires, our hopes, our dreams, our total and utter dependence upon God, fearing God with every breath and with every thought. Total brokenness is the only way to completion and wholeness.

Individually we must be obedient to His design. He has designed us to be in close covenant within a local church body. Bible studies and prayer groups are not churches. They are "parts" of a church. Individually, we are commanded to "know" those who labor amongst us. We are commanded to test the fruit. We are to be breaking bread and meeting regularly throughout the week as the first century church that grew together in wisdom and power. Individually we are to know the word and sharpen each other within the context of who God is more than what the culture is.

Legalism is wrapped up in worshipping God without relationship, and has nothing to do with the ten Commandments! Jesus will not on Judgment day say, "You obeyed my word too much, away with you!" He may say you worshipped me with your lips but your heart was far from me. He may refer to you with the following reference.

> Matthew 17:17 Then Jesus answered and said, O faithless and perverse generation, how long shall I be with you? How long shall I suffer you? Bring him here to Me.

Faith is closely connected and rooted in obedience. A faithless generation is rooted in disobedience and rebellion. We must exercise our faith because of our love for His word. In other words, many of the Pharisees were bound in faithlessness. Also, many within our culture of church are also concreted into faithlessness because of their rebellion to the whole word of God. We must learn to love all of God's word, and we must quit looking at what it will always cost us and emphasize what we will gain.

> Matthew 18:4 Therefore whoever shall humble himself like this little child, this one is the greater in the kingdom of Heaven.

Humility allows us to love what He loves and hate what He hates. Lawlessness commands for Him to love what I love, and hate what I hate. I become a god unto myself. The issues in our culture are rooted in lawlessness. Issues with the churches are rooted within lawlessness. It's time for us to humble ourselves, count the cost, pay the price and rise up with Christ.

Lawless (rebellious) children push family away. Bastard (spiritual) children push the local family (church) away. They bounce from place to place and never belong anywhere. They jump from mentor to mentor never really submitting to those who God placed in our lives to be accountable to and mentored through.

Repent and dig into God. We don't need more self-help seminars until we first are saturated with God's presence through His word, prayer and fellowship. Discipleship is the method God wants to use to transform people's lives. People in a society that craves information over relation, will seek to treat symptoms of gaining information by attending a financial, marriage, addiction, divorce or whatever is lacking in a "self-help" conference. These aspects of life should be developed and discipled within the close-knit covenant of the local church body. Spiritual mentoring (discipling) within our churches doesn't exist anymore, because people again go to church rather than being the church. We don't submit to one another because we don't have true fellowship with one another. We can't disciple one day a week. We can't covenant with a one-day-a-week church. We can't disciple if we stay within our age groups, or married groups, or college ministries. It's okay to have these if the other days of the week we are with the rest of the people.

The best Bible Study I ever attended was made up of people of all ages that I covenanted with throughout the week. My wife and I were one of the youngest couples there. The range expanded out to people over 40 years older and spiritually more mature than we were. Studying with this diverse group was the only way I was going to mature. When I began to submit, God began to move in my life by doing signs and wonders, delivering, healing and the like in others within the group. People from all over were hearing of the "WOW!" that God was doing in our midst.

We must choose to deepen our roots in Christ in a local on-fire church that is open seven days a week with opportunities to be all we can be in Christ. Mentoring and Discipleship would train our "children."

> Proverbs 22:6 Train up a child in the way he should go; and when he is old, he will not depart from it.

This means our physical children, but I also believe we can extend it to our spiritual children we are mentoring towards Christ. Bastard children, whether physical or spiritual, don't want this. They would rather go to a seminar to learn what they should be learning by submitting to those within a covenant relationship, or read a self help book in the privacy of their own darkness. We are commanded to carry one another's burdens. This is again about relationship and covenant.

We have a culture of non-relational churches, first small and now large, that do church well, providing great music, well-taught presenters and events for all ages. But, what our culture of church lacks is Jesus. We talk about Him, the Father and the Holy Spirit, but are they allowed to direct the flow and outcomes? Do we esteem each other more than we do ourselves if we don't even know the people we are near?

It is time for a culture change. It's time to have a revival that begins in our hearts and is contagious to those in our sphere of influence. Today's a wonderful day for it to happen. Why Not?!

Questions to ponder:

1. Do you attend a Biblical, legalistic or law-less church? Match the heart of the people with the heart and actions of Christ. Are they about rules without relationship? Are they about relationships without submissive obe-

dience, or do they love to submit unto God's laws and one unto another?

2. What steps can you take to become relational on a daily basis to God, your church and the Body of Christ?

3. To be like Christ means to love His Fathers laws and commandments. Do you love to obey the Word or do you use greasy-grace to water down your faith and reap the consequences of disobedience into your life and your family line?

4. If our churches would preach the whole word and use discipleship, we wouldn't need specific self-help topical studies (or at least as much). Do you belong to a church that emphasizes multi-generational and gendered group studies that allow for individuals and married alike to attend? Or, do you individualize and segregate every group on to its own "island"?

Chapter 13

Redeeming the

Bastard Culture

I**T'S TIME FOR THE CHURCH TO LIVE** Jesus. Live Jesus out loud! We do need to make best marriages through the power of Jesus Christ. It's time for us to be great servants to our communities and beyond! It's time for us to be the best stewards of our finances and belongings! We do these things through relational, covenant discipleship.

Some may feel I am against big churches. No! I am just against taking a dead ritual, putting new paint on it, making it big, adding a bunch of bells and whistles, hiring some professional musicians who may or may not be saved, tell them to do good things, meet once a week and call it good. When are we going to leave dead religion and live out Christ's mandates He set while He was on earth. Anything else is illegitimate.

We have replaced His presence with atmosphere. I have been asked by many people (not knowing I am a pastor of a church) to come to their church. They brag of the music, pastor, children and youth ministries, or whatever. But, I have never been told that the presence of God shows up and people start repenting, transformation occurs or the like. How sad it is that we worship the stuff and not His presence and power. His presence is the best present we will ever get.

We define the churches purpose, just like the world wants to redefine the marriage. We already have created a Church that allows people to soak in their sins, be in the world and of the world and not set apart, live lawless lives flavored with fornication, adultery, lust, drunkenness, idolatry, murder, fantasy, violence, selfishness, divorce, homosexuality, lying and perversity. The list could go on. No, sin hasn't been done away with, only the eternal damnation if we repent by asking for forgiveness and turning away from it and running.

The church no longer fears God! We don't love what He loves and hate what He hates. We want to control the Spirit. Things like healing, raising the dead, casting out demons, dreams and visions are easily pushed aside by programs and logic. No wonder the lion of this world is stealing, killing and destroying the people in the church. They are powerless in his schemes. Their families are being destroyed by doctrines of demons and of men. The church is walking in illegitimacy. We are without the Father! We accept the Son because even criminal gangs understand brotherhood to death. What we need is the Father that protects and shelters His children. So, then we also need the Holy Spirit. He is Jesus' gift to us. Just as Jesus was empowered by Him, so must we. Jesus didn't just cleanse our temple for salvation, but for impartation of power, holiness and divine passion. Fear Him in love and power. Chase after Him! Don't ask "what can I do and still be saved?" Ask the Lord "what can I give up, to get closer to you?" Salvation wasn't just for you. It was for His longing to have fellowship with His image bearers. Most people focus on the "Thou shall nots," but we should be focusing on the "Thy will be dones." We are more worried about what we can't do than what we can now do through the power of Jesus Christ and the Holy Spirit. As a wise man said, "I must give up my dignity, for His Deity."

It is now that we prepare ourselves to meet our Groom - Jesus Christ. As with Esther, this took a full year to do using perfumes and bathing. A time of being set apart from the commoners and the former life. If you want the blessings of a Christian life you must "come out of her" - the world that is. Esther had a mission from God. The only way it could be accomplished was to prepare herself to be with the king. God has a plan for our lives. The only way we can find Godly success and our destiny is to prepare to meet with the King ... not someday but today! Marriage has always been at the front of God's plan and destiny for mankind. As mentioned earlier in the book, we live in a fatherless culture. Even when a father is present in the home he usually isn't. He's busy with his hobbies, video gaming and sports. We have a Father wanting a relationship with us and we reject Him. No wonder the devil saturates us with rejection - we are reaping what we are sowing! Push God the Father away and the step-father of this world steps in to destroy the children. Do you know that statistics show that by far most abuses occur through the step-parent? While there are good ones out there, God never intended for the "step-lifestyle" to occur. There is no such thing as a spiritual vacuum. Either God the Father is there or the godfather of this world is there, creating illegitimacy and division within the family, both the physical and spiritual families.

We must present great marriage leadership through strong marriages. We need to reach out to the actual children born out of wedlock and allow the transformational power of the Holy Ghost to change their DNA from unwanted and unloved to fulfilled and destined for victories. Fornication and sexual perversities are breeding grounds that foster generational garbage and curses to fester for a life time. This leads to creating more "Bastard" children because you can reproduce only who and what you are.

We live in radical times. It is now time for radical warriors to rise-up and represent Christ well. Fight the good fight! Finish well! Don't run to dungeons of our hearts or the tombs of our churches to "worship" the God whom our hearts are far from the other six days and 22 hours. Going to church only two hours a week is less dedicated than going to the bathroom or eating or sleeping. We must be the church especially when it isn't popular, and specially when it is hard! Rise up church! Come out of your slumber. Become the home and family the world is looking for.

Radical times take radical measures to offset the symptoms. If you just found out that you have stage four cancer, what would you do? Would you go on as if nothing were wrong? Would you choose to fight or would you flight out of there? Would you go to a bigger hospital because there are more people there? What would you do?

Bastard children need adoptive parents with stable homes and clear ditches that are well defined. Spiritual children need the same. They need a stable home church and people they are in covenant with. They don't need "Big Brother" or "Big Sister" programs. They need a "Big God" program rooted in Godly love and fellowship twenty-four seven.

It's sad to see that people with this bastard mentality are always running away from something, rather than running to what they need. It used to be said that daughters would marry someone similar to their father, or sons would marry someone similar to their mother. Now, the curse has young men and women chasing after things trying to fill the holes of lacking fathers and mothers within their lives. Again, spiritual children are the same way, always searching but never finding. They are never content, only disenfranchised.

My hope is that this book is a fresh revelation of the heartbeat of the body of Christ. It is an overview of the trend and current symptoms of the "heart-failure" we are experiencing. Just like every prognosis by a doctor or specialist is fine tuned to the patient's needs, the local church knows its needs and people (we hope). Any outsider that comes in must build a community of relationship and fellowship custom designed by the Designer to restore "family" in the Body.

Do you feel left out? Do you feel abandoned? Do you feel unloved? Do you feel rejected? Do you crave for a man or woman by your side? Were you birthed outside of the covenant of marriage? Were you conceived outside of the covenant of marriage? Were you an unwanted pregnancy? If so, then worthlessness, rejection and abandonment may rule your life. Let Jesus reverse the curse placed over you and your future.

Do you find yourself constantly offended and church hopping? Are you uncommitted to other believers within the Body? Does reading these symptoms irritate you, and do find yourself making excuses? Do you find yourself indifferent when it comes to church, bible study and prayer? Do you find yourself attracted to non-believers more than believers? (The way you spend your time is evidence of that.) Do you find yourself going to church more than being the church? Do you find fault in every church you go to? Do you struggle with shame, guilt and condemnation? Do you always see what the problem is, but are unwilling to apply yourself to be part of the answer? Do you find that your life lacks the power, signs and wonders and miracles of a Christ-centered life? Do you lack the fruit of the Spirit and the Gifts of the Spirit in your everyday life?

If any of these apply to you, then you may be experiencing a Bastard curse! Find an on-fire church, full of the Spirit. Find a church that is rooted in your community and ministers twenty-four seven. Get rooted in. Repent of your judgmental and critical spirit. Let your roots run deep. Overflow in the fruit and gifts of the Spirit. Meet as close to daily as you can. Let iron sharpen iron. Hang out daily with mentors exploding with passion for the Gospel and the wisdom of God. Create a well-rounded personal and corporate life of worship. Seek after the Kingdom of God and His righteousness, and all the rest will fit into place. Be consumed by God's fire, and the world's fires won't consume you. As for me and my house, we will serve the Lord in Spirit and in Truth!

SO, YOU SAY YOU CAN'T! I SAY TO YOU:

WHY NOT?!

Prayer:

*Almighty God, I repent of any curse
I may have placed upon myself because of sin that I have chosen. I
break off any curse that my parents,
grandparents or any other relation
may have allowed going back a hun-
dred generations. Lord, I repent of
the rebellion and lawlessness that
has stolen my past and my present. In
the name of Jesus, I refuse to let it
steal my future. My future is rooted
in the victories of Jesus Christ, and I
am a new creation. I am His beloved.
I am a child of the King. I am beau-
tifully and wonderfully made with
purpose and a destiny of goodness
through Jesus Christ. No weapon
formed against me shall prosper. I
am a co-heir with Christ. I have been
grafted in, and adopted into a royal
heritage. I am His ambassador. My
weapons are not of this world. I fight
with spiritual weapons that pull down
every stronghold. Greater is the
Jesus within me through the Holy
Spirit than he who is in the world. I
release the Holy Spirit to unleash a
consuming fire of righteousness and*

holiness within me. I ask for purification and impartation of His fullness
to break me and remake me. Nothing
is impossible for God, and therefore
I can do all things through Christ
who strengthens me. Just as God has
blessed me with an earthly family and
life, He has also given me opportunity
to be a spiritual family.

The body of Christ is vast as well
as local. I choose to be in a Bible-
preaching church that accepts the
whole Bible as Truth. I choose this
day to chase after my God with those
He has placed around me. I choose
not to get offended but to be loving
and let grace and mercy abound. I refuse any longer to have a club mentality. Church was meant to be a twenty-
four seven, three-sixty-five worship
experience with Him and those in my
immediate church family extending
outward. I choose the life of Christ.
I will no longer be an illegitimate
child - physically or spiritually. I belong to the King, His Kingdom and His
family. I can walk with power to exercise the Fruit of the Spirit and give
testimony as Jesus and His followers
through the gifts of the Spirit. I will
not have a form of Godliness. I will
not deny the power of the Gospel
Jesus lived, preached and taught.

I will walk humbly and boldly pro-
claiming the Gospel in word, deed,
action and power. I choose to focus
my eyes upon the author and finisher

of my faith. I will run the good race, fight the good fight and finish the race well. Not by my might, nor my power, but by His Spirit. If I should stumble and fall, I will, through the power of His Spirit, get back up and continue running. I will read the Word, pray, fellowship, worship, gather with other believers daily as the first-century church exampled for us to do. It was here that signs and wonders followed those who believed. They added and even multiplied to their numbers - sometimes daily.

Lord, help me love You, seek You with all my heart, worship You, hear Your voice, obey without hesitation, pour myself out as an offering, walk in tune with the Spirit, allow your power to overflow and touch others. It is my pleasure to call you Daddy and King. Jesus, You are my friend, savior and Lord. I welcome the day when You say "Welcome My son, My good and faithful servant. Great is your reward. Come on in here and let's get this party started." I am His child. I am His creation. I am made in His image. I am HIS!

In Jesus name, I dedicate my life, this prayer and all that I will ever be. AMEN!

Don't try to do this alone. Get in a Bible-preaching and living church that follows in Jesus' footsteps by doing what He did, and where they meet throughout the week for prayer, Truth and encouragement. Find a church that isn't focused upon 'self-help,' but is about brokenness and restoration through the blood of Jesus Christ. Find a church that equips the people for the ministry of the Gospel. This is probably the last generation of church as we know it. People partaking of the current "churchy" atmosphere will probably not return to one that preaches sin, repentance, holiness, daily gathering together of the Body, individual and corporate growth and the covenant relationship of each member.

But, out of this current demise will rise the remnant church. They will seek after God twenty-four seven. They will be both hearers and doers of the Word. They will hunger and thirst after righteousness. They will strive to surround themselves with others who are on fire for Jesus and allow Him to speak through the Word, dreams/visions, and prophecy. Now go into all the earth and proclaim the gospel in word and miraculous actions through the delegation of Jesus and the empowerment of the Holy Spirit. It's all about relationships with Him, and with others. Radical times call for a radical God to be released upon a world that needs His Hope and Truth. See you in heaven!

About the Author

Author, Wayne North, resides in Wisconsin with his wife, six children and 1 grandchild. Wayne has been working in ministry since 1992. He currently is the senior pastor of FREEDOM Community Church. His passion is for the church to regain its First love once again, and for it to become the righteous and purified bride of Christ. Wayne's mission is for the church to flow in the miraculous power of the Holy Ghost. Wayne believes it's time for the Church to walk in the footsteps of Jesus Christ and to demonstrate the Kingdom principles as it brings the hope and transformational power of the Gospel to the dark world. His hope is that the Church would once again use the Biblical blueprint of the "Five Fold" (or "Four Fold" as some designate) ministry to equip and empower the people to do the ministry of the Gospel especially in the areas of the apostolic, prophetic and evangelistic. He enjoys seeing the power of the Holy Ghost bring salvation, healing, deliverance and other signs and wonders to transform people's lives and ruin nice religion for the comfortable. Wayne's hobbies include coaching football, hunting and fishing. His background as a science teacher and farmer have helped him make the Gospel real and relevant in his teachings and discipleship.

www.ingramcontent.com/pod-product-compliance
Lightning Source LLC
Chambersburg PA
CBHW031534040426
42445CB00010B/537